GOSPEL QUESTIONS, GOSPEL ANSWERS

BY BEST-SELLING AUTHOR

DAVID J. RIDGES

Books by David J. Ridges

The Gospel Studies Series

- *Isaiah Made Easier, Second Edition*
- *The New Testament Made Easier, Part 1, Second Edition*
- *The New Testament Made Easier, Part 2, Second Edition*
- *Your Study of The Book of Mormon Made Easier, Part 1*
- *Your Study of The Book of Mormon Made Easier, Part 2*
- *Your Study of The Book of Mormon Made Easier, Part 3*
- *Your Study of The Doctrine and Covenants Made Easier, Part 1*
- *Your Study of The Doctrine and Covenants Made Easier, Part 2*
- *Your Study of The Doctrine and Covenants Made Easier, Part 3*
- *The Old Testament Made Easier, Part 1*
- *The Old Testament Made Easier—Selections from the O.T., Part 2*
- *The Old Testament Made Easier—Selections from the O.T., Part 3*
- *Your Study of the Pearl of Great Price Made Easier*
- *Your Study of Jeremiah Made Easier*
- *Your Study of The Book of Revelation Made Easier, Second Edition*
- *Gospel Studies Series Deluxe Sets*

Additional Titles by David J. Ridges

- *Our Savior, Jesus Christ: His Life and Mission to Cleanse and Heal*
- *Mormon Beliefs and Doctrines Made Easier*
- *The Proclamation on the Family: The Word of the Lord on More Than 30 Current Issues*
- *65 Signs of the Times and the Second Coming*
- *Doctrinal Details of the Plan of Salvation: From Premortality to Exaltation*
- *To This End Was I Born: Walking with the Savior in His Final Week*
- *Temples: Sacred Symbolism, Eternal Blessings*
- *Priesthood Power Unlocked*
- *Using the Signs of the Times to Strengthen Your Testimony*
- *The Red Porsche*
- *The Righteous Role of a Father*
- *A Mother's Perfect Hope*
- *Seasons of a Mother's Love*
- *Born to the Virgin Mary*

GOSPEL QUESTIONS, GOSPEL ANSWERS

BY BEST-SELLING AUTHOR
DAVID J. RIDGES

CFI
AN IMPRINT OF CEDAR FORT, INC.
SPRINGVILLE, UTAH

ISBN 13: 978-1-4621-2006-2

Published by CFI, an imprint of Cedar Fort, Inc.
2373 W. 700 S., Springville, UT, 84663
Distributed by Cedar Fort, Inc., www.cedarfort.com

LIBRARY OF CONGRESS CATALOGING-IN-PUBLICATION DATA ON FILE

Cover design by Shawnda T. Craig
Cover design © 2017 Cedar Fort, Inc.
Edited and typeset by Heather Holm

Printed in the United States of America

10 9 8 7 6 5 4 3 2 1

Printed on acid-free paper

CONTENTS

CONTENTS

INTRODUCTION

This book contains 100 questions about the gospel and 100 corresponding answers that come from trustworthy sources. I have been asked these questions a number of times by students in my classes over my many years of teaching seminary, institute, adult religion, and in other Church settings, as well as during my time as a bishop and stake president. Misunderstanding on some of these issues has caused anxiety, frustration, and sadness, sometimes for many years. Occasionally, it has led to inactivity or leaving the Church. Upon receiving answers based on correct doctrine, burdens have been lifted and peace and hope have replaced feelings of discouragement and doubt.

The format of this book is simple. The questions are listed in the table of contents in random order. Readers are invited to browse through the questions until they find one that raises curiosity or is already a question of interest, and then go to the specified page in the book where that question is addressed.

The answers are kept relatively brief and come from the scriptures, the words of modern prophets, and Church publications that include general conference talks, manuals, resources on the Church's website, and talks and writings of Church leaders.

GOSPEL QUESTIONS, GOSPEL ANSWERS

1

Question: If I attain exaltation, do I have to live plural marriage?

Answer: No.

Over the course of my many years of teaching in the Church, including in seminary, institute, and adult religion classes, several of my students, especially the sisters, have asked me this question. Often, it has been because of discussions in classes they have attended in church during which the teacher or another student taught that if women expect to gain exaltation, they must get used to the idea of living plural marriage. This is an unfortunate and damaging false doctrine that has caused much anxiety and conflict between testimony and compliance. Sometimes men who take pleasure in making women uncomfortable teach this false idea. In effect, they are exercising "unrighteous dominion" (D&C 121:39) over their women counterparts in the Church.

Elder Bruce R. McConkie taught the following regarding this subject:

Plural marriage is not essential to salvation or exaltation. Nephi and his people were denied the power to have more than one wife and yet they could gain every blessing in eternity that the Lord ever offered to any people. In our day, the Lord summarized by revelation the whole doctrine of exaltation and predicated it upon the marriage of one man to one woman (D&C 132:1–28). Thereafter he added the principles relative to plurality of wives with the express stipulation that any such marriages would be valid only if authorized by the President of the Church (D&C 132:7, 29–66). (Mormon Doctrine [Salt Lake City: Bookcraft, 1966], p. 578)

In the Book of Mormon, Jacob taught his people that the Lamanites, whom the Nephites despised, were more righteous than they regarding how they were treating their wives. In so doing, he reminded them of the commandment of the Lord given to Lehi that they were to have one wife and no concubines (second class or servant wives).

Jacob 3:5

5 Behold, the Lamanites your brethren, whom ye hate because of their filthiness and the cursing which hath come upon their skins, are more righteous than you; for they have not forgotten the commandment of the Lord, which was given unto our father—that they should have save it were **one wife, and concubines they should have none**, and there should not be whoredoms committed among them.

Sometimes misunderstanding regarding plural marriage here in mortality, as well as in exaltation in eternity, arises from misreading Doctrine and Covenants, section 132. Verses 3–33 refer to the law of celestial marriage and the specific covenants and principles that are associated with it. These apply to anyone who is worthily sealed in the temple by proper priesthood authority and do not refer to plural marriage. Verses 34–66 are an appendage to this revelation regarding plural marriage. If people become confused and apply verses 34–66 to all who enter into celestial marriage, sad misunderstanding and false doctrines regarding plural marriage can and do arise.

2

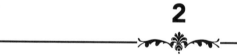

Question: Will there be some who live plural marriage in exaltation?

Answer: Yes.

The Lord made it clear that, under certain circumstances, He commands plural marriage.

Jacob 2:27, 30

27 Wherefore, my brethren, hear me, and hearken to the word of the Lord: For there shall not any man among you have save it be **one wife**; and **concubines** [*second class or servant wives*] he shall have **none**;

30 For if I will, saith the Lord of Hosts, raise up seed unto me [*if I want to have large, righteous families quickly*], I will command my people [*to practice plural marriage*]; otherwise they shall hearken unto these things [*the commandment given in verse 27*].

In such cases, if they are worthy and desire it, these husbands and wives will live together as families in eternity.

Also, many of us know worthy men who lost their first wife to whom they were sealed in the temple. They later remarried and were sealed to another wife. Thus, many righteous husbands will enter eternity with more than one wife.

And if a righteous wife in that circumstance does not want to live in such a situation, we can understand, from the Father's plan of happiness for each of His children, that no worthy woman will be forced, against her will, to live in a situation in which she would be unhappy. Joseph Smith said, "Happiness is the object and design of our existence" (*Teachings of the Prophet Joseph Smith* [Salt Lake City: Deseret Book, 1977], p. 255). It is wonderful that we have the entire Millennium for such things to be worked out to every worthy person's complete satisfaction.

3

Question: When temple-married parents are divorced, who are the children sealed to?
Answer: Children are not resealed in this life.

Many people fail to put this question in the proper eternal context and thus worry unnecessarily. If you stop and think about it, when we finally enter exaltation, we will all be resurrected adults. This includes the children whose status brought up this question in the first place. We will be married for eternity to our spouses. We will be sealed in our own eternal family unit. Beyond that, we will be sealed in all directions to everyone in the family of Adam and Eve who now dwell in the highest degree of the celestial kingdom (exaltation). The sealings are in the form of a "net" rather than in a straight line. Everyone there is sealed to everyone else, so the problem of which parent the children are sealed to is solved. It no longer exists.

Example 1

Let's say a couple was married in the temple, had three children, and then divorced. Over time, both parents remarry someone else and do what is necessary to be worthily sealed to their new spouses. All three children grow up and marry in the temple. The Second Coming occurs, the Millennium finishes, and the time for the Final Judgment has arrived. At this point, both parents and their spouses are worthy of exaltation. It's the same with the three children who married in the temple. All of them are now judged worthy of continuing in their own family units throughout eternity as gods, and they do. Their main involvement is now in their own eternal family unit, having spirit children, creating worlds for them to go to in order to obtain physical bodies, and so forth. They are also all sealed to everyone else from this world who attained exaltation, including their parents, grandparents, and on and on (if they proved worthy of exaltation). It is just like in the case of extended pedigree charts. If you go back far enough, in one way or another, everyone eventually ends up related to everyone else.

Example 2

A couple was married in the temple, had three children, and then divorced. Over time, both parents remarry and are sealed to their new spouses in the temple. All three children grow up. Two marry in the temple. One does not. Ultimately, the Second Coming occurs, the Millennium finishes, and the time for the Final Judgment has arrived. At this point, both parents and their spouses are worthy of exaltation. The same is true for the two children who married in the temple. All are now judged worthy of continuing in their own family units throughout eternity, and they do. But the child who chose not to become worthy and be sealed in the temple will not be exalted.

In summary, the sealing blessings apply to all in exaltation and no one there is left out. All there are sealed to everyone else there in the family of Adam and Eve. It is like a net of sealings, as in a pedigree chart going in every possible direction—forward, backward, and sideways.

Going back to our original question, if both parents fail to qualify for exaltation but the grandparents or great-grandparents (or other family members back in the genealogical line) do, the sealing of the worthy children will include them. But the child (who is now an adult) who chose not to comply with the law for obtaining exaltation will not be sealed to the family and will remain separate and single throughout eternity (D&C 132:15–17).

4

Question: Can Satan tempt little children?
Answer:　No.

The Lord is clear on this.

D&C 29:46–47

46 But behold, I say unto you, that **little children are redeemed from the foundation of the world through mine Only Begotten**;

47 Wherefore, they cannot sin, for **power is not given unto Satan to tempt little children, until they begin to become accountable before me**.

The Lord also explains when little children begin to become accountable.

D&C 68:25

25 And again, inasmuch as parents have children in Zion, or in any of her stakes which are organized, that teach them not to understand the doctrine of repentance, faith in Christ the Son of the living God, and of baptism and the gift of the Holy Ghost by the laying on of the hands, when **eight years old**, the sin be upon the heads of the parents.

The implication of this wonderful doctrine that Satan cannot tempt little children is that parents and others have the first chance to influence them. Satan has restrictions placed on him by God, and this is one of them.

So, one might ask, why can little children sometimes do naughty things? There are probably several answers. One answer might be environmental influences. Another might simply be that they are strong personalities in little bodies and have the basic character traits of most people.

The point is that Satan is not allowed to tempt them directly, but TV can, family dynamics can, unwholesome environments can, and so forth.

5

Question: To what extent are adultery and fornication forgivable?
Answer: Completely.

A great example of such complete forgiveness is found in the life of Alma the Elder. When we first meet him in the Book of Mormon, he is one of several wicked priests in King Noah's court when the prophet Abinadi is brought before them. Wicked King Noah had done away with all of the righteous priests put in place by his father and replaced them with wicked men who would go along with him in his evil lifestyle (Mosiah 11:5). Noah and his priests are described as being involved in several forms of wickedness, including sexual immorality.

Mosiah 11:6, 14

6 Yea, and thus they were supported in their laziness, and in their idolatry, **and in their whoredoms** [*sexual immorality*], by the taxes which king Noah had put upon his people; thus did the people labor exceedingly to support iniquity.

14 And it came to pass that he placed his heart upon his riches, and he spent his time in riotous living with his wives and his concubines; and **so did also his priests spend their time with harlots** [*prostitutes*].

When Abinadi preached in King Noah's court, Alma was listening. He believed the words of Abinadi and was converted. When the King commanded that Abinadi be put to death, at the peril of his own life, Alma pled with the King to spare the Prophet's life. Sure enough, the King sent servants to find and kill Alma (Mosiah 17:1–4), but he escaped.

Long story short, Alma repented completely and was forgiven. He led his group of faithful followers to the land of Zarahemla, where they joined King Mosiah's people (Mosiah 24:20–25). There, under the direction of King Mosiah, Alma became the President of the Church (Mosiah 25:19). We know he was completely forgiven because the Lord, Himself, told him that he would receive eternal life, which is exaltation in the highest degree of glory in the celestial kingdom and means becoming gods (see D&C 132:19–20).

Mosiah 26:20

20 Thou art my servant; and **I covenant with thee that thou shalt have eternal life**; and thou shalt serve me and go forth in my name, and shalt gather together my sheep.

Another example of complete forgiveness for sexual immorality is found with Alma the Younger's son Corianton, who, while serving a mission, became involved with a prostitute named Isabel. Alma counseled Corianton on how serious such a sin is.

Alma 39:3–5

3 And this is not all, my son. Thou didst do that which was grievous unto me; for thou didst forsake the ministry, and did go over into the land of Siron among the borders of the Lamanites, after the harlot Isabel.

4 Yea, she did steal away the hearts of many; but this was no excuse for thee, my son. Thou shouldst have tended to the ministry wherewith thou wast entrusted.

5 Know ye not, my son, that these things are an abomination in the sight of the Lord; yea, **most abominable above all sins save it be the shedding of innocent blood or denying the Holy Ghost**?

As Alma continued to counsel his wayward son, he invited him to repent so he could ultimately enter the kingdom of God.

<u>Alma 39:9, 12–14</u>

9 Now my son, I would that ye should **repent and forsake your sins**, and go no more after the lusts of your eyes, but cross yourself [*change your* ways] in all these things; for except ye do this ye can in nowise inherit the kingdom of God. Oh, remember, and take it upon you, and cross yourself in these things.

12 And now the Spirit of the Lord doth say unto me: Command thy children to do good, lest they lead away the hearts of many people to destruction; therefore **I command you, my son, in the fear of God, that ye refrain from your iniquities**;

13 That ye **turn to the Lord with all your mind, might, and strength**; that ye lead away the hearts of no more to do wickedly; but rather **return unto them, and acknowledge your faults and that wrong which ye have done**.

14 Seek not after riches nor the vain things of this world; for behold, you cannot carry them with you.

Next, Alma preaches Christ to Corianton, that he might have hope for redemption from his tragic sins.

<u>Alma 39:15–16</u>

15 And now, my son, I would say somewhat unto you concerning the coming of **Christ**. Behold, I say unto you, that it is he that **surely shall come to take away the sins of the world**; yea, he cometh to declare glad tidings of salvation unto his people.

16 And now, my son, this was the ministry unto which ye were called, to declare these glad tidings unto this people, to prepare their minds; or rather that salvation might come unto them, that they may prepare the minds of their children to hear the word at the time of his coming.

Corianton obviously followed his father's counsel, repented, and in due time returned to his missionary labors. Next, we see and feel the precious fact that the Lord's Atonement cleansed and healed Corianton completely of his grievous transgression. Later, in the book of Alma, Mormon points out several faithful servants of the Lord, including Corianton, whom he compares to righteous Captain Moroni.

Alma 48:17–18

17 Yea, verily, verily I say unto you, **if all men had been, and were, and ever would be, like unto Moroni, behold, the very powers of hell would have been shaken forever**; yea, the devil would never have power over the hearts of the children of men.

18 Behold, **he was a man like unto Ammon**, the son of Mosiah, yea, and even the other sons of Mosiah, yea, **and also Alma and his sons, for they were all men of God**.

The Apostle Paul taught that sexual immorality is completely forgivable. As he taught the Corinthian members of the Church, he mentioned these sins, along with a number of other serious sins that can keep us out of the kingdom of heaven unless we repent.

1 Corinthians 6:9–11

9 Know ye not that **the unrighteous shall not inherit the kingdom of God**? Be not deceived: **neither fornicators** [*sexual intercourse between unmarried males and females*], nor idolaters, **nor adulterers** [*sexual intercourse between a man and a woman who are married but not to each other*], nor effeminate, **nor abusers of themselves with mankind** [*male homosexuals*],

10 Nor thieves, nor covetous, nor drunkards, nor revilers, nor extortioners, **shall inherit the kingdom of God**.

Next, Paul teaches that even though some of them had been involved in serious transgression, including sexual immorality (see verse 9, above), they were now forgiven, or could be, and could become clean and pure, worthy to enter heaven if they continued on this path.

11 **And such were some of you**: but **ye are washed** [*baptized*], but ye are **sanctified** [*made pure, holy, and fit to be in the presence of God*], but ye are **justified** [*ratified and approved by the Holy Spirit of Promise, which is the Holy Ghost (see D&C 132:7 and 19) to be exalted*] in the name of the Lord Jesus [*through the Atonement of Christ*], and by the Spirit of our God [*by the Holy Ghost*].

Elder Richard G. Scott taught,

If you have repented from serious transgression and mistakenly believe that you will always be a second-class citizen in the kingdom of God, learn that is not true. The Savior said: "Behold, he who has repented of his sins, the same is forgiven, and I, the Lord, remember them no more. By this ye may know if a man repenteth of his sins—behold, he will confess them and forsake them" (D&C 58:42–43).

Find encouragement in the lives of Alma the Younger and the sons of Mosiah. They were tragically wicked, yet their full repentance and service qualified them to be considered as noble as righteous Captain Moroni (Alma 48:17–18). ("The Path to Peace and Joy," October 2000 general conference)

Just a final thought. One thing that can be problematic for faithful members who have thoroughly repented of serious sin is that when they remember their past transgressions, for which they have indeed seriously repented, they still hurt. They still sting. And if they are not careful, such memories can take over their lives and cause despair and gloom again. Alma the Younger has the answer for this concern.

You will recall that he and the four sons of Mosiah went around seeking to destroy the Church (Mosiah 27:10). They were stopped in their tracks by an angel (Mosiah 27:11–15), and Alma was specifically told to stop persecuting the Church or he would be cast off (or, in other words, be permanently kept out of the presence of God) (Mosiah 27:16).

Years later, as Alma recounted his conversion to his son Helaman, he recalled the deep pain and anguish his sins had caused him.

Alma 36:12–16

12 But **I was racked with eternal torment**, for **my soul was harrowed up** [*torn up*] to the greatest degree and **racked with all my sins**.

13 Yea, I did remember all my sins and iniquities, for which **I was tormented with the pains of hell**; yea, I saw that I had rebelled against my God, and that I had not kept his holy commandments.

14 Yea, and I had murdered many of his children, or rather led them away unto destruction; yea, and in fine so great had been my iniquities, that **the very thought of coming into the presence of my God did rack my soul with inexpressible horror**.

15 **Oh, thought I, that I could be banished and become extinct both soul and body,** that I might not be brought to stand in the presence of my God, to be judged of my deeds.

16 And now, **for three days and for three nights was I racked, even with the pains of a damned soul.**

But then Alma remembered his father's words about Christ and turned to Him. After he repented, allowed his sins to be paid for by the Atonement of Christ, and was cleansed and healed, Alma tells us what became of the sting, pain, anguish, and despair that were the aftermath of his willful sins. Pay attention to the beautiful words used to describe the feelings that replaced the torment in his whole being and brought light and peace to his soul.

Alma 36:17–25

17 And it came to pass that as I was thus racked with torment, **while I was harrowed up by the memory of my many sins,** behold, **I remembered also to have heard my father prophesy unto the people concerning the coming of one Jesus Christ, a Son of God, to atone for the sins of the world.**

18 Now, as my mind caught hold upon this thought, **I cried within my heart: O Jesus, thou Son of God, have mercy on me,** who am in the gall of bitterness, and am encircled about by the everlasting chains of death.

19 And now, behold, when I thought this, **I could remember my pains no more;** yea, **I was harrowed up by the memory of my sins no more.**

20 And oh, **what joy,** and **what marvelous light** I did behold; yea, **my soul was filled with joy** as exceeding as was my pain!

21 Yea, I say unto you, my son, that there could be nothing so exquisite and so bitter as were my pains. Yea, and again I say unto you, my son, that on the other hand, **there can be nothing so exquisite and sweet as was my joy.**

22 Yea, methought I saw, even as our father Lehi saw, God sitting upon his throne, surrounded with numberless concourses of angels, in the attitude of singing and praising their God; yea, and **my soul did long to be there.**

23 But behold, my limbs did receive their strength again, and I stood upon my feet, and did manifest unto the people that I had been born of God.

24 Yea, and from that time even until now, I have labored without ceasing, that I might bring souls unto repentance; that I might bring them to taste of **the exceeding joy of which I did taste**; that they might also be born of God, and be filled with the Holy Ghost.

25 Yea, and now behold, O my son, the Lord doth give me **exceedingly great joy** in the fruit of my labors.

And, finally, I remember the message President Hugh B. Brown gave us missionaries on this topic many years ago at a conference in the Austrian Mission. As near as I can remember, from a journal entry I made at the time, he taught,

Do not insist on remembering what God is willing to forget. The way we are facing is more important than where we are standing. If God is good enough to give us the gift of repentance, we should turn our backs on the past and resolutely face the future unafraid. (From a personal journal entry by David J. Ridges, Austrian Mission)

This is marvelous counsel and fits perfectly with the word of the Lord in the Doctrine and Covenants.

D&C 58:42–43

42 Behold, **he who has repented of his sins, the same is forgiven**, and **I, the Lord, remember them no more.**

43 By this ye may know if a man repenteth of his sins—behold, he will confess them and forsake them.

6

Question: How serious is sexual immorality?
Answer: Next to murder in seriousness.

Regarding sexual immorality, Alma told his son Corianton:

<u>Alma 39:5</u>

5 Know ye not, my son, that these things [*sexual immorality*] are an abomination in the sight of the Lord; yea, **most abominable above all sins save it be the shedding of innocent blood or denying the Holy Ghost**?

Satan has achieved a major goal in our day by convincing large numbers of people that breaking the law of chastity is not a sin. It has become so common that it is considered normal life. Unless we are well grounded in the word of God, we, too, could easily fall into this way of thinking. God's word will always be valid, even when large numbers of people violate His commandments.

Let's look at the commandments relating to sexual purity, and then we will consider some "whys." By the way, promoting the violation of God's laws relating to the law of chastity is one of the major tools used by the devil throughout history to destroy civilizations.

One thing we know for sure. Our Father in Heaven gives us commandments to protect us and make our lives as pleasant as possible, rather than, as some people think, to make us miserable. His laws and commandments are the "rule book" for the most satisfying and rewarding outcome for our lives here on earth, as well as in eternity. We will now discuss a few of the commandments regarding chastity. They teach that sexual immorality is against the laws of God and thus is dangerous to our souls.

<u>Exodus 20:14</u>

14 **Thou shalt not commit adultery**.

1 Corinthians 6:9–10

9 Know ye not that **the unrighteous shall not inherit the kingdom of God**? Be not deceived: **neither fornicators**, nor idolaters, **nor adulterers**, nor effeminate, **nor abusers of themselves with mankind** [*homosexual behavior*],

10 Nor thieves, nor covetous, nor drunkards, nor revilers, nor extortioners, **shall inherit the kingdom of God.**

Mosiah 13:22

22 **Thou shalt not commit adultery**. Thou shalt not steal.

D&C 42:24

24 **Thou shalt not commit adultery**; and he that committeth adultery, and repenteth not, shall be cast out.

Speaking of unrepentant sinners who will ultimately end up in telestial glory, the Lord said,

D&C 76:103

103 These are they who are liars, and sorcerers, and **adulterers**, and **whoremongers** [*those who revel in sexual immorality and make it a consistent focus in their lives*], and whosoever loves and makes a lie.

One of the reasons given in the scriptures as to why sexual immorality of any kind is dangerous to our souls is found in the Doctrine and Covenants. Simply stated, lustful thinking drives the Spirit away. Thus, sexual immorality in any form is dangerous to our spiritual well-being and leaves us vulnerable to Satan's influence.

D&C 42:23

23 And **he that looketh upon a woman to lust after her** shall deny the faith, and **shall not have the Spirit**; and if he repents not he shall be cast out.

Also, among other obvious reasons, sexual transgression is abuse of the very powers of procreation by which innocent life is brought into mortal existence. It is tampering with the life and agency of another of God's spirit children in a way that violates his or her agency to be born into a stable home formed by marriage between a man and a woman. It pollutes the wellsprings of life that are to be reserved, by commandment from God, for the bringing of innocent spirits into mortal existence.

Yet another aspect of why sexual activity outside of marriage between a man and a woman is wrong is the emotional damage and baggage that are left behind because of such involvements. A guilty conscience because of such activities can blunt and diminish the enjoyment and energy for much else in life that would otherwise bring joy and satisfaction.

One critical thing to remember, as stated in this book under the question "To what extent are adultery and fornication forgivable?" is that sexual sin can be forgiven completely, and when it has been forgiven, the sting will be gone, even though the memory can still be retrieved. The sting is gone because, under the comfort and warmth of the Holy Ghost, in conjunction with the Atonement of Christ, it no longer represents who you are. The comfort that comes as a result of deep repentance is one of the functions of the Holy Ghost as the "Comforter" (John 14:16).

The Apostle Paul gave a beautiful description of how this works. His description in the verses quoted next deals with baptism, but it applies also to the results of sincere repentance. Pay close attention to his careful use of highly descriptive vocabulary words as he teaches that when we are baptized, we, in effect, bury our old sinful selves with Christ in the grave. Then, we come forth with Christ as new people, "born again," starting a new life of dedication to the gospel and personal righteousness, which brings a whole new world of opportunity and possibilities for joy, satisfaction, and happiness.

<u>Romans 6:3–5</u>

3 Know ye not, that so **many of us** as **were baptized into Jesus Christ** were baptized into his death [*are you aware that those of us who have been baptized were baptized so that Christ's death, resurrection, and so forth could cleanse us*]?

4 Therefore **we are buried with him by baptism into death** [*being buried in the waters of baptism is symbolic of accepting Christ's invitation to join Him in burying our old sinful selves and thus let our sinful ways die*]: **that like as Christ was raised up from the dead** by the glory of the Father, even **so we also should walk in newness of life** [*so that just as Christ came forth from the grave in glory, we can come forth from the waters of baptism into a new life filled with the glory and influence of the Father*].

5 For **if we have been planted** [*buried*] **together in the likeness of his death** [*if we have buried our old sinful lives through His Atonement*], **we shall be also in the likeness of his resurrection** [*we will have a glorious new life in the gospel*].

In verse 6, next, Paul uses a strong word to describe the effort sometimes needed on our part to repent of sins. He uses the word "crucify." This implies that it requires much pain and godly sorrow (2 Corinthians 7:9–11) to get rid of some sins. Indeed, changing friends, being cut off from family, going through withdrawals from chemical dependency, confessing a serious sin to the bishop and facing possible consequences, refraining from Sabbath-breaking activities, and cutting back on expenses in order to pay an honest tithe are a few examples of things that can be painful, but walking in "newness of life" (verse 4) makes it far more than worthwhile to "crucify" our sins.

Romans 6:6

6 Knowing this, that **our old man** [*our old lifestyle*] **is crucified with him** [*Christ*], **that the body of sin** [*our past sins*] **might be destroyed**, that henceforth [*from now on*] we should not serve sin.

Sometimes members who have repented from a serious transgression and are active in the Church have trouble listening to talks in sacrament meeting because they remind them of their past sins. For such, the answer is beautifully simple. The talks are no longer addressing their old selves. Rather, their "new selves" are listening, and thus, these topics are now the pleasant and pleasing word of God, to which the person can nod in pleasant agreement and wish that everyone in the world could have the pleasure of adhering to these commandments of God.

7

Question: Can chastity be restored by the Atonement of Christ?
Answer: Yes.

Elder Theodore M. Burton taught,

> Jesus Christ can restore that virtue and he can thus show you mercy . . . **Jesus has power to restore virtue** and make your victim absolutely clean and holy. (BYU Devotional, March 26, 1985)

8

Question: Is it arrogant to plan on exaltation?
Answer: No.

In fact, we are commanded to strive to attain exaltation, which is eternal life in the highest degree of glory in the celestial kingdom. The Savior made it clear that it is a commandment.

Matthew 5:48

48 **Be ye therefore perfect**, even as your Father which is in heaven is perfect.

3 Nephi 12:48

48 Therefore **I would that ye should be perfect** even as I, or your Father who is in heaven is perfect.

Nephi also instructed us to strive for exaltation. If you read his words carefully, in verse 20, next, you will see that it is a commandment.

2 Nephi 31:19–20

19 And now, my beloved brethren, after ye have gotten into this strait and narrow path, I would ask if all is done? Behold, I say unto you, Nay; for ye have not come thus far save it were by the word of Christ with unshaken faith in him, relying wholly upon the merits of him who is mighty to save.

20 Wherefore, **ye must press forward** with a steadfastness in Christ, **having a perfect brightness of hope**, and a love of God and of all men. Wherefore, **if ye shall press forward, feasting upon the word of Christ, and endure to the end**, behold, thus saith the Father: **Ye shall have eternal life** [*which is another phrase meaning exaltation*].

Thus, since we are commanded to become perfect like our Father in Heaven and our Savior, Jesus Christ, and since Nephi says that we "must press forward" with perfect hope toward that goal, it cannot be arrogant. Rather, it is a strong, humble confidence. We should plan on it.

9

Question: How often can we be forgiven of sins?
Answer: As often as we repent.

The simple and beautiful answer from the Lord, Himself, is found in the Book of Mormon.

Mosiah 26:30

30 Yea, and **as often as my people repent will I forgive them their trespasses** against me.

This is comforting and encouraging, since most of us find ourselves repeating many of the same "small" sins over and over in daily life. While we don't want to let ourselves get caught up in rationalizing, nevertheless, there is wisdom in understanding and sincerely accepting the Lord's word on this. Otherwise, we could easily become discouraged and eventually simply give up, deciding that we are just not "celestial material." The idea is to keep trying, to always get up one more time than you fall down. This is how progress is made.

When it comes to the so-called "bigger" sins, including things that would make us unworthy to obtain a temple recommend, the same invitation from our merciful Savior applies. This same invitation appears in various wording throughout the scriptures. Some examples follow.

Isaiah 1:18

18 **Come now, and let us reason together,** saith the LORD: **though your sins be as scarlet, they shall be as white as snow; though they be red like crimson, they shall be as wool.**

Jacob 6:4–5

4 And **how merciful is our God** unto us, for he remembereth the house of Israel, both roots and branches; and **he stretches forth his hands unto them all the day long** [*inviting them to repent*]; and they are a stiffnecked and a gainsaying people; but as many as will not harden their hearts shall be saved in the kingdom of God.

5 Wherefore, my beloved brethren, I beseech of you in words of soberness that ye would **repent,** and come **with full purpose of heart,** and cleave unto God as he cleaveth unto you. And **while his arm of mercy is extended towards** you in the light of the day, harden not your hearts.

10

Question: Is active homosexuality against God's commandments?
Answer: Yes.

Notice that the question says "active" homosexuality. Having feelings of same-sex attraction is not a sin any more than having attraction toward the opposite sex is. The sin comes in becoming actively involved in physical same-sex relations. Those who have same sex attraction but control it and keep it within proper bounds are basically the same as those who are sexually attracted to members of the opposite sex but control their feelings and keep them within the bounds that God's laws require. In both cases, Alma's counsel to his son Shiblon applies.

Alma 38:12

12 Use boldness, but not overbearance; and also see that ye **bridle all your passions**, that ye may be filled with love; see that ye refrain from idleness.

Notice that in order to be morally clean, we are not required to "extinguish" our passions, but rather to "bridle" them, or, in other words, keep them under control.

The Bible places homosexuality in the same category as adultery and fornication. In the last chapter of the book of Revelation, the Bible specifies some sexual sins that, unrepented of, would keep a person out of the celestial kingdom. These include male homosexuality and heterosexual immorality.

Revelation 22:15

15 For without *are* **dogs** [*A reference to male prostitutes for men. See* The Living Word, *by Luther A. Weigle (New York: Thomas Nelson & Sons, 1956).*], and sorcerers, and **whoremongers** [*people who frequently chase after sexual satisfaction outside of marriage*], and murderers, and idolaters, and whosoever loveth and maketh a lie.

Likewise, Moses specifies active homosexuality, whether among men or women, as being against God's laws.

Deuteronomy 23:17–18

17 There shall be no whore of the daughters of Israel [*among the daughters of Israel*], nor a **sodomite** [*Deuteronomy 23:17, footnote b, 1989 LDS Bible, "a professional male or female prostitute, or cultist. TG Homosexuality"*] of the sons of Israel.

18 Thou shalt not bring the hire of a whore [*the wages earned by a female prostitute*], or the **price of a dog** [*A reference to wages earned by male prostitutes for men. See* The Living Word, *by Luther A. Weigle (New York: Thomas Nelson & Sons, 1956).*], into the house of the LORD thy God for

any vow: for even both these *are* abomination unto the LORD thy God. *[An equivalent today might be, "You can't pay tithing on wages you earn as a prostitute or a homosexual prostitute."]*

In the book of Romans, in the Bible, the Apostle Paul warned against some of the worst sins being committed by people in Rome at the time, including sexual immorality in many different forms, such as masturbation, lesbianism, and homosexuality. See the heading to chapter 1 in our LDS Bible where it confirms that Paul is referring to homosexuality. See also Topical Guide, under "Homosexuality" for additional references to the sin of homosexual behavior.

We will add some explanatory notes to these verses, including some definitions from *Strong's Exhaustive Concordance of the Bible*, by James Strong (New York: Hunt & Eaton, 1890).

Romans 1:24–28

24 Wherefore God also gave them up *[allowed them to use their agency and thus turned them over]* to uncleanness *[immorality]* through the lusts *[evil, immoral desires]* of their own hearts, to **dishonour their own bodies between themselves** *[by themselves; see Strong's #1722; in other words, masturbation]*:

25 Who changed the truth of God into a lie *[they changed the righteous use of the power of procreation into perversion]*, and worshipped and served the creature *[lusts of the flesh]* more than the Creator, who is blessed *[is to be praised]* for ever. Amen.

26 For this cause *[because they desired wickedness]* God gave them up unto vile affections *[because of agency, God allowed them to become involved in depraved passion; see* Strong's #3806*]*: **for even their women did change the natural use** *[of the powers of procreation]* **into that which is against nature** *[perversion; see Strong's #5449]*: *[In other words, women got involved in lesbianism, homosexuality, and so forth. See McConkie,* Doctrinal New Testament Commentary *(Salt Lake City: Bookcraft, 1966), 2:220.]*

27 And likewise also the men *[the men did similar things]*, leaving the natural use of the woman *[departing from normal, proper sexual relations with their wives]*, **burned in their lust one toward another** *[became inflamed with sexual attraction toward other men]*; **men with men**

[*homosexuality; see Romans 1:27, footnote a*] **working that which is unseemly** [*shameful; involving nakedness; see* Strong's *#0808*], and receiving in themselves that recompence of their error which was meet [*required by God's laws; in other words, setting themselves up for the punishment of God for their perversion*].

28 And even as they did not like [*choose*] to retain God in their knowledge [*to acknowledge God's laws*], God gave them over to a reprobate mind [*allowed them to exercise their agency leading toward failing the test*], to do those things which are not convenient [*which are improper*].

Unfortunately, the world has, for the most part, discarded the Bible as the moral reference for laws and standards of acceptable behavior. It is easy to see why Satan has made this a major goal for his attacks on society and against the gospel of Christ, since the Bible has been one of the major hurdles standing in his way.

In summary, a prophet of God has clearly stated the Lord's position on this issue. President Gordon B. Hinckley taught,

We believe that marriage between a man and a woman is ordained of God. We believe that marriage may be eternal through exercise of the power of the everlasting priesthood in the house of the Lord.

People inquire about our position on those who consider themselves so-called gays and lesbians. My response is that we love them as sons and daughters of God. They may have certain inclinations which are powerful and which may be difficult to control. **Most people have inclinations of one kind or another at various times. If they do not act upon these inclinations, then they can go forward as do all other members of the Church.** If they violate the law of chastity and the moral standards of the Church, then they are subject to the discipline of the Church, just as others are.

We want to help these people, to strengthen them, to assist them with their problems and to help them with their difficulties. But we cannot stand idle if they indulge in immoral activity, if they try to uphold and defend and live in a so-called same-sex marriage situation. To permit such would be to make light of the very serious and sacred foundation of God-sanctioned marriage and its very purpose, the rearing of families. (Gordon B. Hinckley, "What Are People Asking about Us?" October general conference, 1998)

11

Question: What if one "blows" his or her patriarchal blessing?
Answer: All is not lost.

On occasions, after receiving a patriarchal blessing, the recipient departs from the path required to earn a particular blessing stated in it. This is what we mean when we say a "blown" patriarchal blessing. When this happens, the person might feel that all is lost. It isn't. The Lord loves us. His Atonement is still available. Even if that particular blessing at a given time in our lives is not going to be fulfilled, we can still repent, grab hold of the iron rod, and move ahead to other blessings in our lives. We can still have the ultimate goal and promise from God that we can attain the highest happiness and blessings available that lead to exaltation in our own celestial family units in the highest degree of glory in the celestial kingdom.

Example 1

A young man is told in his patriarchal blessing that, if he remains worthy and strives to prepare for a mission, he will be called to a mission field where he will do much good and find much satisfaction. But, in the course of his later teens, he becomes inactive in the Church, gets involved in drugs, and then in selling drugs, and ends up in prison for twelve years. He can still repent, but he is not going to serve a mission as a young elder. However, if he repents thoroughly and gets his life on the gospel track, he and his wife can serve several senior missions and derive joy and satisfaction in so doing. All is not lost. The past is left behind and the future is completely bright!

Example 2

Another young man is likewise told in his patriarchal blessing that if he remains worthy, he will be called on a mission. However, in the course of his later teens, he goes steady with his girlfriend and she ends up pregnant. They get married. The baby is born, and the young couple determines to be active and faithful in the Church so the baby has a gospel-centered home. In due time, they are sealed in the temple as a family.

The part of his patriarchal blessing in which he was told to prepare for a mission as a young elder will obviously not be fulfilled. But all is not lost. Indeed, the future is bright, including happiness on earth and the prospect of exaltation in the highest degree of glory in the celestial kingdom.

Example 3

A young woman is told in her patriarchal blessing that, if she strives for it and is worthy, she will, in the Lord's due time, grow in love with a righteous son of God, and they will be sealed for time and eternity in a temple of the Most High. However, in her later teens, she starts skipping church and Young Women, runs around with some wild friends, including boys, and, in the course of a little over a year, decides to elope to Las Vegas where she is married to a nonmember young man. He doesn't really have a job but has promised to get one. Their parents provide some help, but the thrill of marriage and independence soon wears off. In time, she finds that she is expecting their baby. Her husband starts spending a lot of time with his old friends, and what she thought was love turns out to be shallow infatuation. In despair, one day she digs out her patriarchal blessing and reads it. Sadly, that sends her into deeper depression.

But still, all is not lost. The invitation to repent and do what we can to get our lives in order is still there for her. It may take time, even a long time, with much effort and even putting up with a lot of disappointment. But with the help and guidance of the Lord through the Holy Ghost, she still has all of the blessings of eternal family and exaltation before her, even if it takes until the Millennium is underway to get things in place for these blessings.

Example 4

A young woman is promised temple marriage in her patriarchal bless-ing, based on her worthiness and striving for it, but she marries outside the Church. She and her husband have several children and a reasonably satisfying marriage. He is a good provider but shows no interest in the Church. She begins attending church and gradually becomes active. Even-tually, tension begins to build between them. He spends more time away from their home and family and becomes somewhat emotionally abusive toward her. She tries to improve the marriage but it doesn't work. She decides against divorce for the sake of the children and simply endures.

She finally decides to receive her own endowment, if he will give his permission. He does, but still rejects anything to do with the Church. Over time, the children grow up, marry, and leave home. Her relationship with her husband remains somewhat friendly but cool. She remains active in the Church but worries that her choices earlier in her life will prevent her from ever having an eternal family.

One day, as she does her regular reading in her Book of Mormon, she is struck by two verses in the book of Jacob. The Spirit causes certain words to, in effect, "jump off the page" as she reads.

Jacob 6:4–5

4 And how merciful is our God unto us, for he remembereth the house of Israel, both roots and branches; and **he stretches forth his hands unto them all the day long**; and they are a stiffnecked and a gainsaying people; but as many as will not harden their hearts shall be saved in the kingdom of God.

5 Wherefore, my beloved brethren, I beseech of you in words of sober-ness that ye would **repent, and come with full purpose of heart**, and cleave unto God as he cleaveth unto you. And **while his arm of mercy is extended towards you in the light of the day**, harden not your hearts.

This starts her wondering if there is still hope for her for having an eternal marriage. The Spirit gives her a warm feeling, but she doesn't know how it could ever happen. Some months later, during her regular Book of Mormon reading time, some words again jump off the page.

Mosiah 26:30

30 Yea, and **as often as my people repent will I forgive them their trespasses against me**.

And the Spirit gives her warmth and hope that it is still not too late. Her thinking changes from despairing of ever having an eternal family of her own to that of actually planning, quietly to herself, with simple faith, for someday having this blessing.

In a way, Joseph Smith's situation with the lost 116 manuscript pages is similar to someone whose behaviors preclude the fulfillment of promised blessings in a patriarchal blessing. From Joseph's experience, we are taught that all is not lost.

You may recall that Joseph was translating from the golden plates in Harmony, Pennsylvania, with Martin Harris as his scribe. Martin was under intense pressure and ridicule from his wife and acquaintances back home in the Palmyra, New York, area, who were spreading rumors that Martin was being duped and taken advantage of by Joseph Smith. His wife feared that Joseph would get all of Martin's money. In desperation, Martin asked if he could take the manuscript pages back home and show them to his wife and critics to calm their fears and stop their wagging tongues.

Joseph asked the Lord for permission to let him take them but was told no. Martin asked him to ask again. He did, and was again told no. Martin kept at it, and, finally, Joseph asked again, upon which the Lord said yes, if Martin would promise to show the 116 pages to only five people, including his wife and four others. Martin was ecstatic, took them, and left. But he did not keep his promise and showed them to others. The 116 pages were lost. Martin was devastated. Joseph was devastated.

And here's where a comparison to a "blown" patriarchal blessing might be made. In a way, it might be said that Joseph Smith had a "patriarchal blessing" in which he was told that he would translate the Book of Mormon from the golden plates. In the course of translating, young Joseph made a serious mistake when he yielded to pressure from Martin Harris. Martin was twenty-two years older than Joseph and was serving as a scribe. Joseph let him take the 116 pages of translated manuscript. Martin did not keep his promise, and the 116 pages were lost. The angel came to Joseph and took the plates and the Urim and Thummim. Then shortly after, the angel appeared again and gave him the Urim and Thummim. Joseph received what we know as section 3 of the Doctrine and Covenants, after which the angel took the Urim and Thummim and left. In this revelation, the Lord chastised Joseph for yielding to the pressure from Martin rather than being faithful to his responsibilities to safeguard the translation of the plates.

D&C 3:5–8, 12–15

5 Behold, you have been entrusted with these things, but how strict were your commandments; and **remember also the promises which were made to you, if you did not transgress them.**

6 And behold, how oft you have transgressed the commandments and the laws of God, and have gone on in the persuasions of men.

7 For, behold, **you should not have feared man more than God.** Although men set at naught the counsels of God, and despise his words—

8 Yet **you should have been faithful**; and he would have extended his arm and supported you against all the fiery darts of the adversary; and he would have been with you in every time of trouble.

12 And when thou deliveredst up that which God had given thee sight and power to translate, **thou deliveredst up that which was sacred into the hands of a wicked man,**

13 Who has set at naught the counsels of God, and has broken the most sacred promises which were made before God, and has depended upon his own judgment and boasted in his own wisdom.

14 And this is the reason that thou hast lost thy privileges for a season—

15 For **thou hast suffered the counsel of thy director to be trampled upon from the beginning**.

In the following verses, Joseph Smith was warned but still given comfort and hope.

D&C 3:9–11

9 Behold, thou art Joseph, and thou wast chosen to do the work of the Lord, but **because of transgression, if thou art not aware thou wilt fall**.

10 **But remember, God is merciful; therefore, repent of that which thou hast done which is contrary to the commandment which I gave you, and thou art still chosen, and art again called to the work**;

11 **Except thou do this, thou shalt be delivered up and become as other men, and have no more gift**.

Continuing with our comparison to a patriarchal blessing, Joseph would not be allowed to "retake" the 116 pages portion of his blessing. But all was not lost. He was able to move forward in his life after a time of serious thinking and repenting. According to his mother, the plates and Urim and Thummim were returned to Joseph on September 22, 1828. (See *The History of Joseph Smith by His Mother*, Lucy Mack Smith [Salt Lake City: Bookcraft, 1958], pp. 134–35.) In a revelation he received at that time, he was told not to redo the translation of the 116 manuscript pages, which were from the large plates of Nephi, but rather to translate the same period of history from a small batch of plates within the golden plates, known as the small plates of Nephi.

D&C 10:1–3

1 NOW, behold, I say unto you, that **because you delivered up those writings** [*the 116 pages*] which you had power given unto you to translate by the means of the Urim and Thummim, into the hands of a wicked man, **you have lost them**.

2 And **you also lost your gift at the same time, and your mind became darkened**.

3 Nevertheless, **it is now restored unto you again**; therefore see that you are faithful and continue on unto the finishing of the remainder of the work of translation as you have begun.

D&C 10:38–41

38 And now, verily I say unto you, that an account of **those things that you have written, which have gone out of your hands, is engraven upon the plates of Nephi** [*the large plates of Nephi*];

39 Yea, and you remember it was said in those writings that **a more particular account was given of these things upon the plates of Nephi** [*the small plates of Nephi*].

40 And now, because the account which is engraven upon the plates of Nephi is more particular concerning the things which, in my wisdom, I would bring to the knowledge of the people in this account—

41 Therefore, **you shall translate the engravings which are on the plates of Nephi** [*the small plates of Nephi*], down even till you come to the reign of king Benjamin, or until you come to that which you have translated, which you have retained.

Thus, while not being able to redo and make right the things relating to the 116 pages, he was allowed and invited to move forward in his life and accomplish the Lord's work in a different way, ultimately leading to his exaltation.

D&C 132:49

49 For I am the Lord thy God, and will be with thee even unto the end of the world, and through all eternity; for verily **I seal upon you your exaltation**, and prepare a throne for you in the kingdom of my Father, with Abraham your father.

Therefore, all is definitely not lost if a portion of a patriarchal blessing cannot be fulfilled because the person did not adhere to the path required for its fulfillment. If that person later returns to the strait and narrow path essential for exaltation in the highest degree of glory in the celestial kingdom, he or she will receive eternal glory and happiness in the family unit and become a god forever.

12

Question: What if a worthy member wants to receive his or her endowment but the spouse doesn't approve?
Answer: There is still hope.

It may require quiet patience, and, perhaps, even waiting until passing through the veil to receive this blessing. Elder Russell M. Nelson taught that some faithful members will have to wait until the next life for the blessing of eternal marriage. And the same principle from the Lord can apply to faithful members who, in order to keep the peace in their marriage, defer receiving their endowment. Elder Nelson taught,

> But what of the many mature members of the Church who are not married? Through no failing of their own, they deal with the trials of life alone. Be we all reminded that, in the Lord's own way and time, no blessings will be withheld from His faithful Saints. The Lord will judge and reward each individual according to heartfelt desire as well as deed. (Russell M. Nelson, October 2008 general conference)

13

Question: How long did it take to create the earth?
Answer: We don't know.

One common answer to this question would be something to the effect that it took six thousand years for the Creation. This is based on the belief that each of the six days of creation lasted a thousand years. This, in turn, is based on the accounts given in Genesis, chapter 1, and in Moses, chapter 2, in which a brief description of each of the "days" of creation is given, coupled with the fact that "one day is with the Lord as a thousand years," as given in 2 Peter 3:8. Putting these scriptures together has led some to conclude that each "day" of creation consisted of one thousand years. We need to be cautious in interpreting the above references so absolutely.

Another frequently heard answer would be millions of years. This would be based on scientific evidence. Yet another answer could be that each day of creation could be however long was needed for the purposes of that period, and they would not necessarily need to be the same.

It is important that we not be caught up in arguments as to how long it actually took to create the earth. We do know for sure that the Lord created it. If you carefully read Genesis, chapter 1, you will see over forty ways in which the Lord says, in effect, "I created the earth." Another important thing to know is that Jesus will give us the answers to these questions and give us more details about the creation of the earth when He comes again, as stated in the Doctrine and Covenants.

D&C 101:32–34

32 Yea, verily I say unto you, in that day **when the Lord shall come, he shall reveal all things—**

33 Things which have passed, and hidden things which no man knew, **things of the earth, by which it was made**, and the purpose and the end thereof—

34 Things most precious, **things that are above, and things that are beneath, things that are in the earth, and upon the earth, and in heaven.**

Apostle Bruce R. McConkie is quoted on this subject in the *Doctrines of the Gospel Student Manual* (used in the institutes of religion of the Church [Salt Lake City: The Church of Jesus Christ of Latter-day Saints, 2000], p. 17) as follows:

But first, what is a day? It is a specified time period; it is an age, an eon, a division of eternity; it is the time between two identifiable events. And each day, of whatever length, has the duration needed for its purposes. . . . **There is no revealed recitation specifying that each of the "six days" involved in the creation was of the same duration.**

Abraham was a great astronomer as well as a prophet. As he described the Creation, he used the term "time," which leaves it open as to how long each day of the Creation was. We will look at some verses from Abraham.

Abraham 4:8, 13, 19, 23, 31

8 And the Gods called the expanse, Heaven. And it came to pass that it was from evening until morning that they called night; and it came to pass that it was from morning until evening that they called day; and this was **the second time** that they called night and day.

13 And it came to pass that they numbered the days; from the evening until the morning they called night; and it came to pass, from the morning until the evening they called day; and it was **the third time**.

19 And it came to pass that it was from evening until morning that it was night; and it came to pass that it was from morning until evening that it was day; and it was **the fourth time**.

23 And it came to pass that it was from evening until morning that they called night; and it came to pass that it was from morning until evening that they called day; and it was **the fifth time**.

31 And the Gods said: We will do everything that we have said, and organize them; and behold, they shall be very obedient. And it came to pass that it was from evening until morning they called night; and it came to pass that it was from morning until evening that they called day; and they numbered **the sixth time**.

In summary, we do not know how long Jesus took to create the earth under the direction of the Father. It is nice to know, however, that someday the Creator Himself will give us the answer.

14

Question: Did others help create the earth?
Answer: Yes.

In the Book of Abraham in the Pearl of Great Price, we see the Savior inviting the "noble and great ones" to help Him create the earth.

Abraham 3:22–24

22 Now the Lord had shown unto me, Abraham, the intelligences [*spirits; see verse 23*] that were organized before the world was; and **among all these there were many of the noble and great ones**;

23 And God saw these souls [*spirits*] that they were good, and he stood in the midst of them, and he said: These I will make my rulers; for he stood among those that were spirits, and he saw that they were good; and he said unto me: Abraham, thou art one of them; thou wast chosen before thou wast born.

24 And there stood one among them that was like unto God [*in other words, the premortal Christ stood among these "noble and great spirits"*], and **he said unto those who were with him: We will go down, for there is space there, and we will take of these materials, and we will make an earth whereon these** [*all of the spirits assigned to this earth*] **may dwell**;

Apostle Joseph Fielding Smith, who became the tenth President of the Church, taught this also.

It is true that **Adam helped to form this earth**. He labored with our Savior Jesus Christ. **I have a strong view or conviction that there were others also who assisted them**. Perhaps Noah and Enoch; and why not Joseph Smith, and those who were appointed to be rulers [*Abraham 3:23*] before the earth was formed? (Joseph Fielding Smith, *Doctrines of Salvation* [Salt Lake City: Bookcraft, 1954], 1:74–75)

15

―――――――――――――

Question: Did we evolve from lower forms of life?
Answer: No, according to the First Presidency.

The First Presidency, Joseph F. Smith, John R. Winder, and Anthon H. Lund, gave the following statement in 1909 regarding the question as to whether we evolved from lower forms of life.

It is held by some that Adam was not the first man upon this earth, and that the original human being was a development from lower orders of the animal creation. These, however, are the theories of men. The word of the Lord declares that Adam was "the first man of all men" (Moses 1:34), and we are therefore in duty bound to regard him as the primal parent of our race. It was shown to the brother of Jared that all men were created in the beginning after the image of God; and whether we take this to mean the spirit or the body, or both, it commits us to the same conclusion: **Man began life as a human being, in the likeness of our heavenly Father.** (*Improvement Era*, November 1909, 13:75–61. See also *Messages of the First Presidency of The Church of Jesus Christ of Latter-day Saints* [Salt Lake City: Bookcraft, 1965–75], 4:205. Also quoted in the Institute of Religion's student manual *Doctrines of the Gospel* [Salt Lake City: The Church of Jesus Christ of Latter-day Saints, 2000], p. 17)

From the same First Presidency statement, we read,

All men and women are in the similitude of the Universal Father and Mother and are literally the sons and daughters of deity . . . "God created man in his own image." This is just as true of the spirit as it is of the body, which is only the clothing of the spirit, its complement; the two together constituting the soul. **The spirit of man is in the form of man, and the spirits of all creations are in the likeness of their bodies**. This was plainly taught by the Prophet Joseph Smith (Doctrine & Covenants 77:2). (The First Presidency: Joseph F. Smith, John R. Winder, Anthon H. Lund, *Messages of the First Presidency*, James R. Clark, compiler [Salt Lake City: Deseret Book, 1970], 4:203)

In a question and answer session, now known as section 77 of the Doctrine and Covenants (referred to in the previous quote), Joseph Smith taught that our spirit is in the form of our bodies, and that the spirits of animals, birds, bugs, and so forth, are in the form of their physical bodies.

D&C 77:2

2 Q. What are we to understand by the four beasts, spoken of in the same verse [*Revelation 4:6*]?

A. They are figurative expressions, used by the Revelator, John, in describing heaven, the paradise of God, the happiness of man, and of beasts, and of creeping things, and of the fowls of the air; **that which is spiritual being in the likeness of that which is temporal; and that which is temporal in the likeness of that which is spiritual; the spirit of man in the likeness of his person, as also the spirit of the beast, and every other creature which God has created.**

We will consider a few other interesting questions relating to the Creation.

Question: Was Eve taken from one of Adam's ribs?

Answer: No.

President Spencer W. Kimball, while quoting from Moses 2:27, gave a clarification about the story of Eve being created from Adam's rib.

And I, God, created man in mine own image, in the image of mine Only Begotten created I him; male and female created I them. [The story of the rib, of course, is figurative.] ("The Blessings and Responsibilities of Womanhood," *Ensign*, March 1976, pp. 71–73)

Knowing that the account is symbolic opens the door to some beautiful imagery and meaning. For instance, Eve was "formed" from an area near Adam's heart, such that they walk side by side, not one ahead of or behind the other. She is protected by his arm (arm is symbolic of power in Biblical culture), and they work together, side by side, in harmony and unity. (Eve is now "bone of my bones, and flesh of my flesh," Genesis 2:23.) Their loyalty to each other is even greater than their loyalty to their parents ("Therefore shall a man leave his father and his mother, and shall cleave unto his wife,"

Genesis 2:24), and they become "one flesh" (Genesis 2:24), symbolizing unity, harmony, enjoying being together as eternal companions, as well as symbolizing bringing children into the world.

Question: Why do the scriptures make the story of the rib sound so literal if it is merely symbolic?

Answer: This is typical of Biblical culture and writing.

We "westerners" (residents of the Western Hemisphere, especially the US and Canada) tend to want things to be literal, and much of our writing and culture reflects this. However, such is not the case with many other cultures, including Biblical and other eastern cultures. Thus, much of their writing is highly symbolic, transferring emotion and feeling as well as fact to the reader. So it is that the scriptural accounts of the creation of Eve give much more than the fact that she came on the scene. They provide drama and feeling, warmth and tenderness, belonging and protectiveness, unity and purpose to the account, far beyond Adam and Eve's coming forth to fulfill their role in the great "plan of happiness" (Alma 42:8).

Question: Was the earth created in its present location in the solar system?

Answer: No.

We understand from the teachings of Brigham Young that the earth was created near where Heavenly Father resides and that it was moved to this particular area of space, into this solar system, at the time of the Fall of Adam and Eve. We will quote Brigham Young here and then add a quote from Joseph Smith.

> This earth is our home. It was framed expressly for the habitation of those who are faithful to God, and who prove themselves worthy to inherit the earth when the Lord shall have sanctified, purified and glorified it and **brought it back into his presence, from which it fell far into space . . . When the earth was framed and brought into existence and man was placed upon it, it was near the throne of our Father in heaven.** And when man fell . . . **the earth fell into space, and took up its abode in this planetary system**, and the sun became our light . . . This is the glory the earth came from, and when it is glorified

it will return again unto the presence of the Father, and it will dwell there, and these intelligent beings that I am looking at, if they live worthy of it, will dwell upon this earth. (Brigham Young, *Journal of Discourses* [London: Latter-day Saints' Book Depot, 1854–86], 17:143)

This earth will be rolled back into the presence of God, and crowned with celestial glory. (*Teachings of the Prophet Joseph Smith* [Salt Lake City: Deseret Book, 1977], p. 181)

16

Question: What if I was called on a mission but had to come home because of illness?

Answer: The future still holds bright promise.

We sometimes tend to think that because God has called us to do something important, all obstacles to our accomplishing it will be removed by the powers of heaven. According to the scriptures, this is not always the case.

D&C 124:49

49 Verily, verily, I say unto you, that when I give a commandment to any of the sons of men to do a work unto my name, and those sons of men go with all their might and with all they have to perform that work, and cease not their diligence, and their enemies come upon them and hinder them from performing that work, behold, **it behooveth me to require that work no more at the hands of those sons of men, but to accept of their offerings**.

The "enemies," mentioned in the verse quoted above, can include illness. We sometimes forget that life is a "curriculum," designed, among other things, to test us and strengthen our loyalty to God regardless of the undesired circumstances in which we find ourselves. Just ask Job in the Old Testament. All kinds of trouble and misfortune came at him even though he consistently chose the right and was obedient to God's commandments. He lost his property, all ten of his children, servants, flocks, and wealth. (See Job, chapter 1; also see heading to chapter 1.) In short, he went from being the wealthiest man in the country to having nothing that would be considered of value in the eyes of his friends and others. His response? He firmly and consistently reaffirmed his loyalty to God.

Job 1:20–21

20 Then Job arose, and rent his mantle, and shaved his head, and fell down upon the ground, and worshipped,

21 And said, Naked came I out of my mother's womb, and naked shall I return thither: **the LORD gave, and the LORD hath taken away; blessed be the name of the LORD.**

After losing all of his precious children, his servants, and all of his vast material wealth, he next lost his physical health and comfort. He was sorely afflicted with boils from head to toe.

Job 2:7

7 So went Satan forth from the presence of the LORD, and smote Job with **sore boils from the sole of his foot unto his crown.**

All this misfortune and misery came upon Job despite his righteous living. Even his wife put pressure on him to confess his sins that had led to such personal disaster and to stop claiming that he had not compromised his integrity with God. (She thought he must have done something wrong to deserve what was happening to him.) Still, he remained loyal and obedient to the Lord.

Job 2:9–10

9 **Then said his wife unto him, Dost thou still retain thine integrity?** [*Are you still claiming you have not committed some grievous sin?*] curse God, and die.

10 But he said unto her, Thou speakest as one of the foolish women speaketh. What? shall we receive good at the hand of God, and shall we not receive evil? **In all this did not Job sin with his lips.**

In chapter after chapter of Job, we read of the trials and difficulties with which he was afflicted through no particular fault of his own. He continues faithful, bearing his testimony, and affirming his loyalty to God.

Job 19:25–27

25 For **I know** *that* **my redeemer liveth**, and *that* he shall stand at the latter *day* upon the earth:

26 And *though* after my skin *worms* destroy this *body,* yet **in my flesh shall I see God**:

27 **Whom I shall see for myself, and mine eyes shall behold**, and not another; *though* my reins be consumed within me.

Job 27:4–5

4 **My lips shall not speak wickedness, nor my tongue utter deceit**.

5 God forbid that I should justify you: **till I die I will not remove mine integrity from me**.

Ultimately, at the end of the book of Job (chapter 42), we see that the Lord rewarded him generously for his faithfulness despite his severe troubles and opposition.

Job 42:10, 12, 13, 16, 17

10 And the LORD turned the captivity of Job, when he prayed for his friends: also **the LORD gave Job twice as much as he had before**.

12 So **the LORD blessed the latter end of Job more than his beginning**: for he had fourteen thousand sheep, and six thousand camels, and a thousand yoke of oxen, and a thousand she asses.

13 He had also seven sons and three daughters.

16 **After this lived Job an hundred and forty years**, and saw his sons, and his sons' sons, *even* four generations.

17 So Job died, ***being* old and full of days**.

The happy and satisfying final outcome for Job at the end of his life could be considered symbolic of all whose lives have had disappointments and unexpected setbacks, despite faithful adherence to God's commandments and despite striving to fulfill callings from Him. It is reassurance from a loving Heavenly Father that the future can still be bright through the grace of Christ.

Perhaps we can mention one more principle that can apply to the missionary who was forced to come home early from a mission because of health concerns. This same principle applies to all members who have not been able to completely fulfill a calling because of health. It is called "the short straw principle."

The Short Straw Principle

Sometimes we try to come up with an explanation or reason why we are not able to complete an assignment from the Lord so we can repent and become worthy, but we really can't find one. It may be simply because there isn't one. We refer to such a circumstance as "the short straw principle," or, in other words, we simply drew the "short straw," so to speak. An example of this is in the Book of Mormon.

You may recall from your studies that the four sons of Mosiah, after their conversion with Alma the Younger (Mosiah 27), went on missions to the Lamanites. There, they split up and went to various territories among the Lamanites. Ammon ended up in King Lamoni's kingdom, where, after being imprisoned and released, he found favor with King Lamoni. The king offered Ammon one of his daughters for a wife. Ammon became a servant to the king. He saved the king's flocks from robbers by cutting off several of their arms and became famous and highly regarded there. He eventually successfully taught the gospel to the king, his wife, and many others (Mosiah 17–19).

In the meantime, his brother Aaron, along with his companions Muloki and Ammah, were cast into prison in the Land of Middoni (Alma 20:2) and there languished in terribly miserable circumstances. The following verse describes their circumstances when Ammon and King Lamoni came to rescue them.

Alma 20:29

29 And when Ammon did meet them he was exceedingly sorrowful, for behold **they were naked, and their skins were worn exceedingly because**

of being bound with strong cords. **And they also had suffered hunger, thirst, and all kinds of afflictions**; nevertheless they were patient in all their sufferings.

The next verse explains the "short straw principle."

Alma 20:30

30 And, **as it happened, it was their lot** to have fallen into the hands of a more hardened and a more stiffnecked people; therefore they would not hearken unto their words, and they had cast them out, and had smitten them, and had driven them from house to house, and from place to place, even until they had arrived in the land of Middoni; and there they were taken and cast into prison, and bound with strong cords, and kept in prison for many days, and were delivered by Lamoni and Ammon.

And so we see that not all things that happen to us are "cause and effect." Rather, some things fall into the category that "It is what it is." Difficult circumstances end up being part of the test to strengthen us and increase our determination to choose to be faithful no matter the circumstances, including having no clue why something unpleasant is happening to us.

17

Question: What is exaltation?
Answer: Eternal life in the highest degree of glory in the celestial kingdom.

Exaltation means attaining the highest degree of glory in the celestial kingdom. It means becoming gods (D&C 132:20). Exaltation is the same life that our Heavenly Parents enjoy. It includes the blessing and satisfaction of being married for eternity and living in our own family units in the presence of Heavenly Father and Jesus Christ in celestial glory forever. It provides the opportunity to have spirit children, raise them, and teach them the plan of salvation. It means creating worlds for them to go to in order to be born and gain physical bodies, and so forth, so they can also have the possibility of becoming like us in the same way we became like our Heavenly Father.

The Doctrine and Covenants explains that there are three degrees of glory within the celestial kingdom, and in order to attain the highest, a person must have a celestial marriage.

D&C 131:1–4

1 **IN the celestial glory there are three heavens or degrees**;

2 And **in order to obtain the highest, a man must enter into this order of the priesthood** [*meaning the new and everlasting covenant of marriage*];

3 And if he does not, he cannot obtain it.

4 He may enter into the other, but that is the end of his kingdom; he cannot have an increase [*cannot become a god and have spirit offspring for eternity*].

The scriptures teach us that there is a great difference between exaltation and the other two degrees of glory within the celestial kingdom. (See end of verse 16, next.)

D&C 132:15–17

15 Therefore, if a man marry him a wife in the world, and he marry her not by me nor by my word, and he covenant with her so long as he is in the world and she with him, their covenant and marriage are not of force when they are dead, and when they are out of the world; therefore, they are not bound by any law when they are out of the world.

16 Therefore, when they are out of the world they neither marry nor are given in marriage; but are appointed angels in heaven, which angels are ministering servants, to minister for those who are worthy of **a far more, and an exceeding, and an eternal weight of glory**.

17 For **these angels did not abide my law; therefore, they cannot be enlarged** [*have spirit children*], but **remain separately and singly, without exaltation**, in their saved condition, **to all eternity**; and from henceforth are not gods, but are angels of God forever and ever.

18

Question: What are the requirements for gaining exaltation?
Answer: The same as for celestial glory, plus having celestial marriage.

As stated above, the requirements are basically the same as those necessary for entry into the celestial kingdom, plus the additional requirement of entering into and being worthy of celestial marriage as explained in D&C 132:19. The requirements for celestial glory are as follows:

D&C 76:50–53

50 And again we bear record—for we saw and heard, and this is the testimony of the gospel of Christ **concerning them who shall come forth in the resurrection of the just** [*"resurrection of the just" is another term for those who gain celestial glory*]—

51 They are they who **(1) received the testimony of Jesus**, and **(2) believed on his name** and **(3) were baptized** after the manner of his burial, being buried in the water in his name, and this according to the commandment which he has given—

52 That by **(4) keeping the commandments** they might be **(5) washed and cleansed from all their sins**, and **(6) receive the Holy Spirit** by the laying on of the hands of him who is ordained and sealed unto this power;

53 And who **(7) overcome by faith**, and **(8) are sealed by the Holy Spirit of promise**, which the Father sheds forth upon all those who are just and true.

We will add some notes for the numbered items in verses 51–53, above.

1. received the testimony of Jesus

The verb "received" denotes action. The action here is that of receiving the gospel into one's life and living in conformity to its commandments and covenants.

45

2. believed on his name

"Belief" in this context is much more than mere acknowledging. It includes actively living the gospel and believing it will lead to salvation because of the Atonement of Christ.

3. were baptized

These people were baptized by immersion by those who had the priesthood authority to do so.

4. keeping the commandments

Keeping the commandments leads to the cleansing expressed in number 5, next.

5. washed and cleansed from all their sins

Although none of us will be perfect in every way at the time we leave this mortal life, by striving sincerely and honestly to keep the commandments, we qualify to be cleansed from all sins by the Atonement of Jesus Christ. We are thus made pure, clean, and worthy to enter into the presence of God. Not only that, but we are also made comfortable in His presence (compare with 2 Nephi 9:14, last half of verse).

6. receive the Holy Spirit

The gift of the Holy Ghost is given at the time of confirmation. He will guide us in all things if we actively "receive" Him into our lives thereafter. By following His promptings, we will be led to greater and greater understanding of the gospel and will be enabled to have the Atonement of Christ active in our lives. This leads to number 7, next.

7. overcome by faith

The foregoing steps lead to overcoming the sins and temptations of the world, through faith in the Lord Jesus Christ, and thus qualify us to receive number 8, next.

8. are sealed by the Holy Spirit of Promise

The Holy Ghost is the "Holy Spirit of Promise." The name comes from the fact that He is the Holy Spirit that is promised by Jesus to His worthy followers after baptism. One of the roles of the Holy Ghost is to seal or ratify ordinances performed here on earth so that they are also binding in heaven. Thus, when a worthy member is "sealed by the Holy Spirit of Promise," it means that he or she has proven worthy of exaltation and is "sealed up" for that blessing.

You may wish to glance back over verses 51–53 and take note of the fact that it is not complicated to qualify for celestial glory. Some people get the notion that being a faithful, active member of the Church is too complex and difficult to understand. In reality, being faithful to God is the simplest of all lifestyles. Even children can do it. (See D&C 68:25–28.) Complexity enters in when people sin and try to ignore it, hide it, or rationalize it away. As stated above, the only additional requirement for exaltation is celestial marriage.

D&C 131:1–2

1 **In the celestial glory there are three heavens or degrees**;

2 And **in order to obtain the highest**, a man must enter into this order of the priesthood [*meaning the new and everlasting covenant of marriage*].

Have you noticed that virtually all of the scriptures and all of the talks and messages from general conferences, Church magazines, regional conferences, stake conferences, sacrament meetings, Church classes, seminary and institute classes, and so forth are focused on helping us obtain exaltation and avoid things that would otherwise detour us to lesser degrees of glory?

If you think about it, you'll notice that you don't hear talks on how to get into the two lower parts of the celestial kingdom. Nor do you hear talks on how to make sure you get into the terrestrial glory, the telestial glory, or even perdition (often referred to as "outer darkness"). No, not at all! Therefore, the answer to this question is that everything we do in the Church is aimed at exalting us. The covenants we make, the ordinances in which we participate, the Atonement of Christ, the gift of repenting, the doctrines we learn, the details of the plan of salvation, church attendance, temple attendance, service opportunities—everything is aimed at getting us back into the presence of God in eternal exaltation.

Again, as mentioned above, the pathway to exaltation is the simplest, least complicated, and most pleasant of all possible paths available to us in mortality. It is indeed simple. Don't deny the Holy Ghost. Don't murder. Don't commit adultery or fornication. Don't steal, lie, or covet. Do go to church. Have faith, repent, and be baptized. Receive the gift of the Holy Ghost to teach you all things and help you stay on the path. And, especially, be nice!

If one chooses to break the commandments of God, life does get more complicated. For example, one who strives to be honest does not have to come up with lies and remember which lies he has already told in order to remain consistent in his fibbing. One who controls her temper does not have to deal with a guilty conscience and be constantly involved in damage control. Those who have a clear conscience do not have to constantly look behind their back for fear that someone is aware of their inappropriate or illicit behavior.

Plenty of trouble comes along our path in the normal course of daily life without our complicating things by breaking the commandments and intentionally ignoring God's counsel as well as ignoring common sense. There is a verse in the Sermon on the Mount that reminds us that daily life has enough trouble without our adding to it by inappropriate or foolish choices.

Matthew 6:34

34 Take therefore no thought for the morrow: for the morrow shall take thought for the things of itself. **Sufficient unto the day *is* the evil thereof** [*in other words, enough trouble will come your way in the course of the day without you intentionally adding to it yourself*].

Nephi gave us strong encouragement to make it to exaltation.

2 Nephi 31:19–20

19 And now, my beloved brethren, after ye have gotten into this strait and narrow path, I would ask if all is done? Behold, I say unto you, Nay; for ye have not come thus far save it were by the word of Christ with unshaken faith in him, relying wholly upon the merits of him who is mighty to save.

20 Wherefore, ye must **press forward** with a steadfastness in Christ, **having a perfect brightness of hope**, and a love of God and of all men. Wherefore, if ye shall press forward, feasting upon the word of Christ, and **endure to the end**, behold, thus saith the Father: **Ye shall have eternal life** [*"eternal life" always means exaltation when it is used in the scriptures*].

Remember, it is through the Atonement of Christ that any of us will make it to exaltation. The Lord's Atonement is what makes the path to exaltation the simplest, most pleasant, and most satisfying path. When we repent quickly as needed in the course of our lives, it makes it possible for us to have joy and be optimists as we strive to continue along the "strait and narrow path" (1 Nephi 8:20).

A verse in the Doctrine and Covenants reminds us that it is through the generous help (grace) of Christ that exaltation is attainable. It reminds us that none of us is perfect, but through the Savior's Atonement, we can make it. This help is available to all. If you understand and believe this teaching, it will give you both humble confidence and strong encouragement to plan on attaining exaltation. It will put a smile on your face many times throughout your life. This verse is referring to those who attain exaltation.

D&C 76:69

69 These are they who are **just men** [*righteous men (and women)*] **made perfect through Jesus** the mediator of the new covenant, who wrought out this perfect atonement through the shedding of his own blood.

19

Question: Will very many people gain exaltation?
Answer: Yes.

The Lord answers this question Himself in the Doctrine and Covenants. Referring to those who will attain exaltation, He states,

D&C 76:67

67 These are they who have come to **an innumerable company of angels**, to the general assembly and church of Enoch, and of the Firstborn [*terms meaning exaltation*].

The Apostle John, whose vision is recorded in the book of Revelation, saw that the number of individuals who will attain exaltation cannot be counted.

Revelation 7:9

9 After this I beheld, and, lo, **a great multitude, which no man could number**, of all nations, and kindreds, and people, and tongues, stood before the throne [*of the Father*], and before the Lamb, clothed with white robes [*symbolic of exaltation*], and palms in their hands [*symbolic of joy, triumph, or victory; in other words, celebrating that they have attained exaltation*].

20

Question: Is there a difference between salvation and exaltation?
Answer: Generally speaking, the answer is no. In some specific contexts, the answer is yes.

First, let's define exaltation. Exaltation is living with our own family unit, becoming gods, and living with Heavenly father and Christ in the highest degree of glory in the celestial kingdom forever. Remember that there are three major degrees of glory. They are, from lowest to highest, the telestial, the terrestrial, and the celestial. In most gospel conversations, when we say "salvation" we are referring to exaltation. In most scripture references, "salvation" means exaltation. The following are some examples.

1 Thessalonians 5:9

9 For God hath not appointed us to wrath, but to **obtain salvation by our Lord Jesus Christ.**

Mosiah 3:18

18 For behold he judgeth, and his judgment is just; and the infant perisheth not that dieth in his infancy; but men drink damnation to their own souls except they humble themselves and become as little children, and **believe that salvation was, and is, and is to come, in and through the atoning blood of Christ, the Lord Omnipotent.**

Alma 34:15

15 And thus **he shall bring salvation to all those who shall believe on his name**; this being the intent of this last sacrifice, to bring about the bowels of mercy, which overpowereth justice, and bringeth about means unto men that they may have faith unto repentance.

D&C 6:13

13 If thou wilt do good, yea, and hold out faithful to the end, thou shalt be saved in the kingdom of God, which is the greatest of all the gifts of God; for **there is no gift greater than the gift of salvation.**

As a side note here, be aware that "eternal life," as used in the scriptures, always means "exaltation."

D&C 14:7

7 And, if you keep my commandments and endure to the end you shall have **eternal life**, which gift **is the greatest of all the gifts of God.**

However, in more specific gospel conversations, discussions, and lessons, there can be a difference. For example, one could refer to "salvation" in the telestial kingdom as opposed to being banished to perdition with the devil and his followers. An example of such use for the term "salvation" is found in the Doctrine and Covenants. In this case, the revelation is explaining some benefits that will come to those consigned to telestial glory.

D&C 76:88

88 And also **the telestial** receive it of the administering of angels who are appointed to minister for them, or who are appointed to be ministering spirits for them; for they **shall be heirs of salvation** [*to the limited degree available in the telestial kingdom*].

The term "salvation," in this case, is used against a backdrop of perdition or "outer darkness," meaning living with the devil and his angels forever. Thus, any final judgment that puts a person anywhere but with the devil would be considered "salvation" indeed.

Reference could even be made to "salvation" in the first degree of glory in the celestial kingdom, but not obtaining exaltation.

D&C 131:1–4

1 **In the celestial glory there are three heavens or degrees**;

2 And **in order to obtain the highest**, a man must enter into this order of the priesthood [*meaning the new and everlasting covenant of marriage*];

3 And **if he does not, he cannot obtain it** [*exaltation*].

4 **He may enter into the other, but that is the end of his kingdom; he cannot have an increase.** [*He cannot be exalted, become a god, have his own family unit, and have eternal increase. (See D&C 132:19.) In other words, he cannot have spirit offspring forever.*]

Thus, he or she would receive a high degree of "salvation," including living with God in celestial glory, but would still fall far short of exaltation, as explained in the following verse.

D&C 132:16

16 Therefore, when they are out of the world **they neither marry nor are given in marriage; but are** appointed **angels in heaven**, which angels **are ministering servants, to minister for those who are worthy of a far more, and an exceeding, and an eternal weight of glory.**

Again, a person could qualify for "salvation" in the terrestrial glory, which might be wonderful compared to telestial glory, but disappointing compared to exaltation in celestial glory.

In summary, the term "salvation" is context sensitive. Most of the time it refers to exaltation, but in certain contexts, it can refer to being saved in a kingdom of glory other than the highest degree of glory in the celestial kingdom.

21

Question: I've heard that there are some lost scriptures and that the Bible is not complete. Is this true?
Answer: Yes.

A number of missing books of scripture are mentioned in the Bible itself. The following is a list taken from the Web on lds.org under "Lost Books."

- Book of the wars of the Lord (Num. 21:14)

- Book of Jasher (Josh. 10:13; 2 Sam. 1:18)

- Book of the acts of Solomon (1 Kgs. 11:41)

- Book of Samuel the seer (1 Chr. 29:29)

- Book of Gad the seer (1 Chr. 29:29)

- Book of Nathan the prophet (1 Chr. 29:29; 2 Chr. 9:29)

- Prophecy of Ahijah (2 Chr. 9:29)

- Visions of Iddo the seer (2 Chr. 9:29; 12:15; 13:22)

- Book of Shemaiah (2 Chr. 12:15)

- Book of Jehu (2 Chr. 20:34)

- Sayings of the seers (2 Chr. 33:19)

- An epistle of Paul to the Corinthians, earlier than our present 1 Corinthians (1 Cor. 5:9)

- Possibly an earlier epistle to the Ephesians (Eph. 3:3)

- An epistle to the Church at Laodicea (Col. 4:16)

- Some prophecies of Enoch, known to Jude (Jude 1:14)

- The book of the covenant (Ex. 24:7), which may or may not be included in the current book of Exodus

- The manner of the kingdom, written by Samuel (1 Sam. 10:25)

- The rest of the acts of Uzziah, written by Isaiah (2 Chr. 26:22)

Thus, the Bible is definitely not complete, and there are indeed many missing scriptures, based on multiple internal evidences within its own pages.

In addition to these references in the Bible, the Book of Mormon also refers to books of scripture that would have existed in Old Testament times that were apparently left out of the Bible. The words of the following three prophets, whose names are found in the verse below, were obviously contained in the brass plates of Laban, which makes them Old Testament prophets. Their written words would logically have been in circulation in other records besides those of Laban.

1 Nephi 19:10

10 And the God of our fathers, who were led out of Egypt, out of bondage, and also were preserved in the wilderness by him, yea, the God of

Abraham, and of Isaac, and the God of Jacob, yieldeth himself, according to the words of the angel, as a man, into the hands of wicked men, to be lifted up, according to **the words of Zenock**, and to be crucified, according to **the words of Neum**, and to be buried in a sepulchre, according to **the words of Zenos**, which he spake concerning the three days of darkness, which should be a sign given of his death unto those who should inhabit the isles of the sea, more especially given unto those who are of the house of Israel.

See also Alma 33:3–17, where Alma refers to Zenos and Zenock.

A great prophecy of Joseph, who was sold into Egypt, is found in Jacob, chapter 3, in the Book of Mormon, but is not found in the Bible.

Furthermore, the Lord makes it abundantly clear, in strong language, that the Bible is not the end of His speaking to His children on earth and that He speaks to all nations and they write it.

2 Nephi 29:6–13

6 **Thou fool, that shall say: A Bible, we have got a Bible, and we need no more Bible**. Have ye obtained a Bible save it were by the Jews?

7 **Know ye not that there are more nations than one?** Know ye not that I, the Lord your God, have created all men, and that I remember those who are upon the isles of the sea; and that I rule in the heavens above and in the earth beneath; **and I bring forth my word unto the children of men, yea, even upon all the nations of the earth?**

8 Wherefore murmur ye, because that ye shall receive more of my word? Know ye not that the testimony of two nations is a witness unto you that I am God, that **I remember one nation like unto another? Wherefore, I speak the same words unto one nation like unto another**. And when the two nations shall run together the testimony of the two nations shall run together also.

9 And I do this that I may prove unto many that I am the same yesterday, today, and forever; and that I speak forth my words according to mine own pleasure. **And because that I have spoken one word ye need not suppose that I cannot speak another; for my work is not yet**

finished; neither shall it be until the end of man, neither from that time henceforth and forever.

10 Wherefore, **because that ye have a Bible ye need not suppose that it contains all my words; neither need ye suppose that I have not caused more to be written.**

11 For **I command all men, both in the east and in the west, and in the north, and in the south, and in the islands of the sea, that they shall write the words which I speak unto them**; for out of the books which shall be written I will judge the world, every man according to their works, according to that which is written.

12 For behold, **I shall speak unto the Jews and they shall write it; and I shall also speak unto the Nephites and they shall write it; and I shall also speak unto the other tribes of the house of Israel, which I have led away, and they shall write it; and I shall also speak unto all nations of the earth and they shall write it.**

13 And it shall come to pass that **the Jews shall have the words of the Nephites,** and the **Nephites shall have the words of the Jews**; and **the Nephites and the Jews shall have the words of the lost tribes of Israel**; and **the lost tribes of Israel shall have the words of the Nephites and the Jews**.

What a "triple combination" that will be!

In conclusion, revelation has not ceased. The Bible is not the only book of scripture available to Heavenly Father's children here on earth. It is not complete. We already have more scripture, including the Book of Mormon, the Doctrine and Covenants, and the Pearl of Great Price. We can look forward eventually, whether in our future, during the Millennium, or at another time, to reading more scripture, including the sealed portion of the Book of Mormon plates. We have on-going revelation through the words of modern prophets and apostles, in written and electronic audio and video formats readily available to us wherever we find ourselves, which has the status of being the word of God and ranks even above scripture in importance.

22

Question: How can we respond to Christians who claim that, according to Revelation 22:18–19, there is to be no additional scripture after the Bible?
Answer: The Bible, itself, gives the answer.

Many missionaries and other members of the Church have been confronted by the argument that the Book of Mormon and other LDS scriptures that are in addition to the Bible violate the commandment of God by adding to the Bible. Often Christian ministers provide lay members of their congregations with Revelation 22:18–19 as "ammunition" against Mormons, especially Mormon missionaries.

Revelation 22:18–19

18 For I testify unto every man that heareth the words of the prophecy of this book, **If any man shall add unto these things**, God shall add unto him the plagues that are written in this book:

19 And **if any man shall take away from the words of the book of this prophecy,** God shall take away his part out of the book of life, and out of the holy city, and *from* the things which are written in this book.

Preferably, in a kind and non-confrontational way, invite them to turn to their Old Testament where they will find a statement similar to that in Revelation 22:18–19 right there in the book of Deuteronomy!

Deuteronomy 4:1–2

1 NOW therefore hearken, O Israel, unto the statutes and unto the judgments [*the word of the Lord, in other words their scriptures, given up to that time through their prophets up to and including Moses*], which I teach you, for to do *them,* that ye may live, and go in and possess the land which the LORD God of your fathers giveth you.

2 Ye shall not add unto the word which I command you, neither shall ye diminish *ought* from it, that ye may keep the commandments of the LORD your God which I command you.

If we were to adhere strictly to a misunderstanding of what the Lord says here, we would be obligated to do away with the rest of the Bible from that verse on!

But, the correct interpretation of what is being said here, as well as in Revelation 22:18–19, is obviously that we should not weaken, discount, selectively cut out portions, or otherwise distort and intentionally change God's word in order to meet our own desires, that of our congregations, or others.

It may also help them to understand that, according to Bible scholars, the Book of Revelation is not the last book written in the New Testament.

When the Apostle John penned the book of Revelation, it was not the last book of the Bible. ("Common Questions about the Book of Mormon," *Ensign*, October 2011, p. 78)

Thus, the warnings in verses 18 and 19 of Revelation, chapter 22, could not be properly interpreted to mean that there should be no more scripture.

23

Question: What if I am still single at the time of the Second Coming?
Answer: You would then only have good people to date.

This question requires a bit of background. Several years ago, in one of my seminary classes, we were having a discussion on the Second Coming of the Savior and the ensuing Millennium. We had just gotten into a rather lively question and answer session when a student near the front of the class excitedly raised his hand and blurted out "I don't want the Second

Coming to come yet!" I asked, "Why?" And he immediately said, "Because I'm not married yet!"

As we continued the discussion, he explained, "You can't get married once the Savior has come and the Millennium has started, and I'm not married yet, so I don't want it to come yet."

I suspect that he had confused our topic with the doctrine that we must be married by the time of the Final Judgment. Otherwise, that ordinance will no longer be available to us. In other words, celestial marriage is an ordinance that must be performed here on earth by mortals, for themselves, or as proxies for those who have died. Doctrine and Covenants section 128, verses 15 and 18, make it clear that mortals must perform the saving ordinances, including baptism and being sealed to spouses and families. (See the next question in this book for more on this.)

So, my student's concern was based on misunderstanding doctrine. We went on to explain that his chances of dating and then marrying someone who was secretly wicked or faking a testimony or whatever, would be nonexistent at the beginning of the Millennium, since all of the wicked would have been destroyed at the Lord's coming. Upon learning this, he grinned and said, "Let the Second Coming arrive and the Millennium begin!"

24

Question: Can resurrected beings do their own temple work since they have a physical body again?

Answer: No.

The scriptures make it clear that the departed dead cannot be saved, or, in other words, gain salvation, unless mortals do proxy ordinances for them in the temples. This is one of God's laws and is one of the ways in which mortals become "saviors on Mount Zion."

D&C 128:15, 18, 22

15 And now, my dearly beloved brethren and sisters, let me assure you that these are principles in relation to the dead and the living that cannot be lightly passed over, as pertaining to our salvation. For their salvation is necessary and essential to our salvation, as Paul says concerning the fathers—that **they without us cannot be made perfect**—neither can we without our dead be made perfect.

18 I might have rendered a plainer translation to this, but it is sufficiently plain to suit my purpose as it stands. It is sufficient to know, in this case, that the earth will be smitten with a curse unless there is a welding link of some kind or other between the fathers and the children, upon some subject or other—and behold what is that subject? It is the baptism for the dead. For we without them cannot be made perfect; **neither can they without us be made perfect**. Neither can they nor we be made perfect without those who have died in the gospel also; for it is necessary in the ushering in of the dispensation of the fulness of times, which dispensation is now beginning to usher in, that a whole and complete and perfect union, and welding together of dispensations, and keys, and powers, and glories should take place, and be revealed from the days of Adam even to the present time. And not only this, but those things which never have been revealed from the foundation of the world, but have been kept hid from the wise and prudent, shall be revealed unto babes and sucklings in this, the dispensation of the fulness of times.

22 Brethren, shall we not go on in so great a cause? Go forward and not backward. Courage, brethren; and on, on to the victory! Let your hearts rejoice, and be exceedingly glad. Let the earth break forth into singing. Let the dead speak forth anthems of eternal praise to the King Immanuel, who hath ordained, before the world was, **that which would enable us to redeem them out of their prison; for the prisoners shall go free**.

In order for this work for the dead to be accomplished, there will need to be a large number of temples. We will continue to build them, until they dot the earth during the Millennium. President Brigham Young said,

To accomplish this work **there will have to be not only one temple but thousands of them**, and thousands and tens of thousands of men and women will go into those temples and officiate for people who have lived as far back as the Lord shall reveal. (Address delivered June 22, 1856, Salt Lake City, Utah; *Journal of Discourses* [London: Latter-day Saints' Book Depot, 1854–86], 3:372)

President Wilford Woodruff reminded us that we will have to do the ordinance work for all of the dead, and it will require the entire Millennium to get it done.

> This work of administering the ordinances of the house of God to the dead I may say, **will require the whole of the Millennium**, with Jesus at the head of the resurrected dead to attend to it. **The ordinances of salvation will have to be attended to for the dead who have not heard the Gospel, from the days of Adam down**, before Christ can present this world to the Father, and say, "It is finished." (September 5, 1869; *Journal of Discourses* [London: Latter-day Saints' Book Depot, 1854–86], 13:327)

25

Question: What is life like during the Millennium?
Answer: Wonderful!

It will be a time of peace and great accomplishment in the work of saving souls. After the destruction of the wicked at the Lord's actual coming, there will only be good people left. This will include many LDS and also many non-LDS whose lives are at least in harmony with the requirements listed in the Doctrine and Covenants for terrestrial glory, such as being honest and pleasant and keeping the law of chastity (D&C 76:72–80). In the course of time, during the Millennium, virtually all will join the Church (D&C 84:98). Untold billions will be born and raised in righteousness. Parents will have great advantages in raising their children during the Millennium.

D&C 45:58

> 58 And the earth shall be given unto them for an inheritance; and they shall multiply and wax strong, and **their children shall grow up without sin unto salvation**.

The government of the world, during the thousand years of peace, will be a "theocracy," which means "government by God." Christ will be at the head of this government as "Lord of lords, and King of kings" (Revelation 17:14).

Bruce R. McConkie described life during the Millennium as follows:

During the millennial era, . . . mortality as such will continue. **Children will be born, grow up, marry, advance to old age, and pass through the equivalent of death.** Crops will be planted, harvested, and eaten; industries will be expanded, cities built, and education fostered; men will continue to care for their own needs, handle their own affairs, and enjoy the full endowment of free agency. Speaking a pure language (**Zeph. 3:9**), dwelling in peace, living without disease. (*Mormon Doctrine* [Salt Lake City: Bookcraft, 1966], pp. 496–97)

Isaiah informs us that there will be no premature death and that people will live to be one hundred years of age during the Millennium.

Isaiah 65:20

20 **There shall be no more thence an infant of days**, nor an old man that hath not filled his days: for the child shall **die an hundred years old**; but the sinner *being* an hundred years old shall be accursed.

A manual used by the Church for institutes of religion confirms this.

In the Millennium children will grow up and live upon the earth until they are one hundred years old. (See Isaiah 65:20; D&C 101:29–31; 63:50–51; 45:58.) (*Doctrines of the Gospel Student Manual*, Rel. 430 and 431 [Salt Lake City: The Church of Jesus Christ of Latter-day Saints, 2004], p. 103)

Men shall die when they are one hundred years of age, and the change shall be made suddenly to the immortal state. (Ibid., p. 104)

Many other details about the destruction of evil at the time of the Second Coming and about life during the Millennium are given in the Doctrine and Covenants.

D&C 101:24–34

24 And **every corruptible thing** [*everything that does not belong in a millennial environment*], both of man, or of the beasts of the field, or of the fowls of the heavens, or of the fish of the sea, that dwells upon all the face of the earth, **shall be consumed**;

25 And also that of element shall melt with fervent heat; and **all things shall become new** [*it will become a paradisiacal earth*], **that my knowledge and glory may dwell upon all the earth**.

26 And in that day the enmity [*animosity*] of man, and the enmity of beasts, yea, **the enmity of all flesh, shall cease** from before my face. [*In other words, it will be a time of great peace.*]

27 And in that day **whatsoever any man shall ask, it shall be given unto him**.

28 And in that day **Satan shall not have power to tempt any man**.

29 And there shall be **no sorrow** because there is **no death** [*as we know it now, such as having funerals, burying our dead, and so forth*].

30 In that day **an infant shall not die until he is old; and his life shall be as the age of a tree** [*one hundred years old*];

31 And **when he dies he shall not sleep, that is to say in the earth, but shall be changed in the twinkling of an eye, and shall be caught up**, and his rest shall be glorious.

32 Yea, verily I say unto you, in that day when **the Lord** shall come, he **shall reveal all things**—

33 Things which have passed, and hidden things which no man knew, things of the earth, by which it was made [*how the earth was created*], and the purpose and the end thereof—

34 Things most precious, things that are above, and things that are beneath, things that are in the earth, and upon the earth, and in heaven.

Did you notice, in verse 28, above, that Satan will not be allowed to even try to tempt people during the thousand years of peace of the Millennium? Joseph Fielding Smith, who became the tenth President of the Church, confirms this pleasant fact.

There are many among us who teach that the binding of Satan will be merely the binding which those dwelling on the earth will place upon him by their refusal to hear his enticings. This is not so. **He will not have the privilege during that period of time to tempt any man**

(D&C 101:28). (*Church History and Modern Revelation* [Salt Lake City: Deseret Book, 1947], 1:192. Quoted in the Institute of Religion's *Doctrine and Covenants Student Manual* [Salt Lake City: The Church of Jesus Christ of Latter-day Saints, 1981], p. 89)

26

Question: If I am alive and married during the Millennium, will I be able to bear children?
Answer: It depends.

The answer is yes, if you and your husband are still mortal. The Doctrine and Covenants states that righteous couples, during the Millennium, "shall multiply and wax strong, and their children shall grow up without sin unto salvation" (D&C 45:58).

The answer is no, as far as having mortal babies is concerned, if you are resurrected and are still here during the Millennium, assisting with the work, and reigning "with Christ a thousand years" (Revelation 20:4). The reason for this answer is that resurrected beings produce spirit offspring, or, in other words, spirit babies, as stated in the Bible and in "The Family: A Proclamation to the World," second paragraph.

Hebrews 12:9

9 Furthermore we have had fathers of our flesh which corrected *us,* and we gave *them* reverence: shall we not much rather be in subjection unto **the Father of spirits**, and live?

Acts 17:28–29

28 For in him we live, and move, and have our being; as certain also of your own poets have said, For **we are also his offspring**.

29 Forasmuch then as **we are the offspring of God**, we ought not to think that the Godhead is like unto gold, or silver, or stone, graven by art and man's device.

The Family: A Proclamation to the World

All human beings—male and female—are created in the image of God. **Each is a beloved spirit son or daughter of heavenly parents**, and, as such, each has a divine nature and destiny. Gender is an essential characteristic of individual premortal, mortal, and eternal identity and purpose. ("The Family: A Proclamation to the World," September 23, 1995; see also *Ensign*, November 1995)

In summary, mortals, of course, produce mortal offspring, whereas, resurrected bodies produce spirit offspring. The only resurrected bodies that will produce spirit offspring will be those of us who receive exaltation. All others will remain separate and single (D&C 132:16–17). Those who do receive exaltation will become gods and will enjoy "a continuation of the seeds forever and ever" (D&C 132:19). In other words, they will have spirit children forever. They will create earths for their spirit sons and daughters to go to and receive mortal bodies and experience the same plan of salvation that our Father is sending us through. (See First Presidency Statement, *Improvement Era*, August 1916, p. 942, which says that those of us who attain exaltation and become gods will use the same plan of salvation that our Father is using for us.)

Those who are mortal and married during the Millennium will have the privilege of bearing children and rearing their families. They will be resurrected when they reach one hundred years of age. Their children will grow up, marry, and have children, and so forth, throughout the Millennium.

Those who are resurrected during the Millennium will no longer have mortal offspring. When the time is right, according to the Lord's plan (we don't know when this will be), they will begin the process of having spirit children (clothing intelligences with spirit bodies through the birth process—see Acts 17:28–29) and loving and rearing them, as our Heavenly Parents did for us.

27

Question: What is the main work of the Millennium?
Answer: Temple work and missionary work.

Have you ever thought how significant it is that the Millennium will require one thousand years? What if it only took two weeks? That would mean that there is not much work left to do. But that is not the case. There will be a tremendous amount of work of salvation still to be done when the Savior comes and ushers in the Millennium. The implication is that many will yet be saved in the kingdom of God. That is happy news!

Temple work and missionary work will be the two main categories of work to be accomplished during the thousand years of peace.

There will be two great works for members of the Church during the Millennium: **temple work and missionary work**. Temple work involves the ordinances that are necessary for exaltation. These include baptism, the laying on of hands for the gift of the Holy Ghost, and the temple or-dinances—the endowment, temple marriage, and the sealing together of family units.

Many people have died without receiving these ordinances. **People on the earth must perform these ordinances for them**. This work is now being done in the temples of the Lord. **There is too much work to finish before the Millennium begins, so it will be completed during that time**. Resurrected beings will help us correct the mistakes we have made in doing research concerning our dead ancestors. They will also help us find the information we need to complete our records. (See Jo-seph Fielding Smith, *Doctrines of Salvation* [Salt Lake City: Bookcraft, 1954–56], 2:167, 251–52.)

The other great work during the Millennium will be missionary work. The gospel will be taught with great power to all people. Eventual-ly there will be no need to teach others the first principles of the gospel because "they shall all know me, from the least of them unto the greatest of them, saith the Lord" (Jeremiah 31:34). (*Gospel Principles* [Salt Lake City: The Church of Jesus Christ of Latter-day Saints, 2009], pp. 13–15)

28

Question: What is it like to be a god?
Answer:　It is the most desirable lifestyle in the universe.

In a seminary class some years ago, we were discussing exaltation, which means life in the highest degree of glory in the celestial kingdom. This includes eternal marriage, becoming gods, and living in our own family units. Near the end of what I thought was a productive and effective discussion, one student, an athletic young man, raised his hand high and emphatically stated, "I don't want to become a god!" That immediately got the whole class's attention, as well as mine. I asked, "Why not?" He replied, "Because I don't want to have to wear a stuffy white shirt, tie, and a black suit all the time and never have any fun!"

Obviously, he had completely misunderstood what it is like to be a god. Joseph Smith taught that gods have the happiest lifestyle of all.

Happiness is the object and design of our existence; and will be the end thereof, if we pursue the path that leads to it; and this path is virtue, uprightness, faithfulness, holiness, and keeping all the commandments of God. (*Teachings of the Prophet Joseph Smith* [Salt Lake City: Deseret Book, 1977], pp. 255–56)

Does this mean that there is no sadness associated with godhood? Of course not! Being gods is eternal parenthood. Our spirit children will have agency, and some will cause sadness when they choose to be disobedient. We are told that the heavens wept when Lucifer was cast out.

D&C 76:25–26

25 And this we saw also, and bear record, that an angel of God [*Lucifer*] who was in authority in the presence of God, who rebelled against the Only Begotten Son whom the Father loved and who was in the bosom of the Father, was thrust down from the presence of God and the Son,

26 And was called Perdition, for **the heavens wept over him**—he was Lucifer, a son of the morning.

But having families eternally brings the highest possible satisfaction and joy. Bearing and raising spirit children, watching them grow and progress, sharing their excitement at discovering things new to them—all of this will bring the highest happiness to parents eternally.

29

Question: Does God have a sense of humor?
Answer: Yes.

This may seem to be an unusual question, but it is an important one. Many people think of God as being stern, strict, quick to punish, always watching for us to make a mistake. Some of this thinking may come as a result of an upbringing as children where parents always threatened that "God can see you, and He will get you if you keep doing that!" or similar such disciplinary threats to children. If we fail to picture God as our kind and loving Father in Heaven, constantly ready to bless and help us, we will lose the opportunity of having a close and tender relationship with Him.

Heber C. Kimball of the First Presidency once said,

I am perfectly satisfied that my Father and my God is a cheerful, pleasant, lively, and good-natured Being. Why? Because I am cheerful, pleasant, lively, and good-natured when I have His Spirit. That is one reason why I know; and another is—the Lord said, through Joseph Smith, "I delight in a glad heart and a cheerful countenance." That arises from the perfection of His attributes; **He is a jovial, lively person, and a beautiful man.** (*Journal of Discourses* [London: Latter-day Saints' Book Depot, 1854–86], 4:222)

30

Question: Why can't people in the terrestrial and telestial kingdoms be married?
Answer: Eternal marriage is reserved for those who attain exaltation.

This answer is in the Doctrine and Covenants.

D&C 131:1–4

1 IN the celestial glory there are three heavens or degrees;

2 And **in order to obtain the highest, a man must enter into this order of the priesthood** [*meaning the new and everlasting covenant of marriage*];

3 And **if he does not, he cannot obtain it.**

4 He may enter into the other, but that is the end of his kingdom; **he cannot have an increase.**

D&C 132:15–17

15 Therefore, **if a man marry him a wife in the world, and he marry her not by me nor by my word**, and he covenant with her so long as he is in the world and she with him, their covenant and marriage are not of force when they are dead, and when they are out of the world; therefore, **they are not bound by any law when they are out of the world** [*in other words, their marriage is dissolved*].

16 **Therefore, when they are out of the world they neither marry nor are given in marriage**; but are appointed angels in heaven, which angels are ministering servants, to minister for those who are worthy of a far more, and an exceeding, and an eternal weight of glory.

17 For these angels did not abide my law; therefore, they cannot be enlarged, but **remain separately and singly**, without exaltation, in their saved condition, to all eternity; and from henceforth are not gods, but are angels of God forever and ever.

Marriage, in the eternal perspective, is far more than companionship for a man and a woman. It is an eternal unit in which intelligences are provided with a spirit body through spirit birth. In this family unit, these spirit children are to be reared and taught the details of the plan of salvation (as was the case for us in our premortality) through which they can, by obedience, become like their heavenly parents. In other words, they can become gods with their own eternal family units. Marriage is reserved for those who qualify to become gods. All others will be separate and single (D&C 132:16–17).

In other words, in order to have the privilege of eternal marriage with the accompanying blessing of "eternal increase" (D&C 132:19), which means having spirit children, a man and a woman must qualify to become gods, which means that they will have become perfect like our Father in Heaven. Anyone who falls short of exaltation, including those in the terrestrial and telestial kingdoms, also falls short of perfection and cannot be gods.

Thus, if residents of the terrestrial or telestial kingdoms were married, it would not be fair to any spirit children born to them to have imperfect and untrustworthy parents. Imagine having a god whom you couldn't trust completely! Some would ask, "Why couldn't they just be married but not have children?" Answer, "Because God said so."

Remember, everything we are taught in the Church and in the scriptures is designed to prepare us for exaltation and to become like our Father in Heaven. We are taught and encouraged constantly to qualify for and enter into celestial marriage. Those who so desire but are not able to attain celestial marriage in this life will have the entire thousand years of the Millennium to achieve it. Thus, any who end up in terrestrial or telestial glory can hardly complain or claim that it is unfair for them to not be married.

31

Question: Why was Satan cast out?
Answer: For rebellion, including wanting to take the place of Heavenly Father.

Isaiah teaches that one of Lucifer's main motives for rebelling was that he wanted to take the place of Heavenly Father. In other words, he wanted to be the "Most High" God. We will add a few notes and commentary to Isaiah's words as he describes Satan's premortal fall from heaven and asks why it happened and what his motives were.

Isaiah 14:12–14

12 **How art thou fallen from heaven** [*Why were you cast out of heaven?*], O Lucifer, son of the morning! How art thou cut down to the ground, which did weaken the nations [*you used to destroy nations; now your power is destroyed*]!

13 For **thou hast said in thy heart** [*these were your motives*], **I will ascend into heaven, I will exalt my throne above the stars of God** [*I will be the highest*]: I will sit also upon the mount of the congregation, in the sides of the north [*mythical mountain in the north where gods assemble*]:

14 I will ascend above the heights of the clouds; **I will be like the Most High.** [*Note that Moses 4:1, quoted below, indicates that he wanted to be the Most High.*]

Be aware that these verses also apply prophetically to the far future, at the end of the Millennium, after the battle of Gog and Magog, when Satan and his followers have been completely defeated and "cast away into their own place" such that they have no more power over us at all (D&C 88:111–14).

In the Pearl of Great Price, we also read that Lucifer wanted Heavenly Father to surrender His power to him, which would mean that he would replace the Father.

Moses 4:1, 3

1 AND I, the Lord God, spake unto Moses, saying: **That Satan**, whom thou hast commanded in the name of mine Only Begotten, is the same which was from the beginning, and he **came before me, saying—Behold, here am I, send me, I will be thy son, and I will redeem all mankind, that one soul shall not be lost**, and surely I will do it; **wherefore give me thine honor** [*which is His power; see D&C 29:36*].

3 Wherefore, because that **Satan rebelled against me**, and **sought to destroy the agency of man**, which I, the Lord God, had given him, and **also, that I should give unto him mine own power**; by the power of mine Only Begotten, I caused that he should be cast down.

32

Question: What happened to the third part of the hosts of heaven who followed Satan in the war in heaven?

Answer: They were cast down to earth and are tempting us here, as well as in the postmortal spirit world prison.

The Bible tells us that they were cast down to earth with the devil.

Revelation 12:7–9

7 And **there was war in heaven**: Michael and his angels fought against the dragon; and the dragon fought and his angels,

8 And prevailed not; neither was their place found any more in heaven.

9 And **the great dragon was cast out**, that old serpent, called the Devil, and Satan, which deceiveth the whole world: he was cast out **into the earth, and his angels were cast out with him**.

These evil spirits are here on earth tempting us and trying to destroy God's work among us. Technically, we are outnumbered, but with God on our side, Satan and his evil followers are effectively outnumbered.

We know from Moses 4:3, quoted in the last question, that a major goal of the devil and his followers is to destroy our agency. Another goal, according to the Book of Mormon, is that the devil wants to make us miserable like he is.

2 Nephi 2:27

27 Wherefore, men are free according to the flesh; and all things are given them which are expedient unto man. And they are free to choose liberty and eternal life, through the great Mediator of all men, or to choose captivity and death, according to the captivity and power of the devil; for **he seeketh that all men might be miserable like unto himself**.

It is interesting to note that these evil spirits can tempt people not only here on earth but also in the prison portion of the postmortal spirit world. Brigham Young taught that these evil spirits cannot tempt the righteous spirits in paradise, but they can tempt those in spirit prison.

If we are faithful to our religion, **when we go into the spirit world**, the fallen spirits–**Lucifer and the third part of the heavenly hosts that came with him**, and the spirits of wicked men who have dwelt upon this earth . . . **will have no influence over our spirits** . . . **All the rest of the children of men are more or less subject to them, and they are subject to them as they were while here in the flesh**. (*Teachings of the Presidents of the Church: Brigham Young* [Salt Lake City: The Church of Jesus Christ of Latter-day Saints, 1977], p. 282)

This makes sense, because those who are hearing the gospel from missionaries in spirit prison have to learn to overcome the temptations of the devil as they strive to learn and live the gospel there, just the same as is the case among us here on earth.

Finally, being cast out of the presence of God in the war in heaven was, in effect, these spirits' final judgment. They, like Satan, will never get a physical body. They, with Satan, will be bound during the Millennium, such that they cannot even try to tempt (D&C 101:28). At the end of the Millennium, they will be let loose for "a little season" to gather all their forces of evil and do battle with Michael (Adam) and all the hosts of the righteous (D&C 88:110–15). This, in scriptural terms, is generally called "the Battle of Gog and Magog" (Revelation 20:8). These evil ones will lose this final battle with righteousness and be permanently banished to perdition (Revelation 17:8), or what is often referred to in gospel discussions as "outer darkness."

33

Question: What do you have to do to become a son of perdition?
Answer: Become like Satan in thought and desires.

The phrase "son of," as in "son of perdition," means "follower of." Thus, "sons of perdition" would mean complete followers of Satan. The Doctrine and Covenants describes those who become such.

D&C 76:31–35

31 Thus saith the Lord concerning all **those who know my power, and have been made partakers thereof**, and **suffered themselves through the power of the devil to be overcome**, and to **deny the truth** and **defy my power**—

32 **They are they who are the sons of perdition**, of whom I say that it had been better for them never to have been born;

33 For **they are vessels of wrath**, doomed to suffer the wrath of God, with the devil and his angels in eternity;

34 Concerning whom I have said there is no forgiveness in this world nor in the world to come—

35 **Having denied the Holy Spirit after having received it**, and having denied the Only Begotten Son of the Father, **having crucified him unto themselves and put him to an open shame**.

We will define descriptive terms and phrases found in verses 31 through 35, above.

1. know my power

In order to "know" God and His power, one must have the witness of the Holy Ghost concerning God and His power. Joseph Smith taught this as follows:

> What must a man do to commit the unpardonable sin? **He must receive the Holy Ghost**, have the heavens opened unto him, and know God, and then sin against him. After a man has sinned against the Holy Ghost, there is no repentance for him. He has got to say that the sun does not shine while he sees it; he has got to deny Jesus Christ when the heavens have been opened unto him, and to deny the plan of salvation with his eyes open to the truth of it; and from that time he begins to be an enemy. This is the case with many apostates of The Church of Jesus Christ of Latter-day Saints. (*Teachings of the Prophet Joseph Smith* [Salt Lake City: Deseret Book, 1977], p. 358)

2. have been made partakers thereof

They are members of the Church and have all ordinances, endowments, etc., that we have available here in this life to prepare for exaltation, as explained by President Joseph F. Smith in the following quote:

> And he that **believes**, is **baptized**, and **receives the light and testimony of Jesus Christ** . . . **receiving the fullness of the blessings of the gospel** in this world, and **afterwards turns wholly unto sin, violating his covenants . . . will taste the second death**. (President Joseph F. Smith, *Gospel Doctrine* [Salt Lake City: Deseret Book, 1977], pp. 476–77)

3. suffered themselves [*allowed themselves, through agency choices*] through the power of the devil to be overcome

In other words, they must intentionally allow themselves to be overcome by Satan.

4. deny the truth

They become absolute liars, completely lacking integrity; or, in other words, they become totally dishonest, like Satan is, denying the truth when they fully know it.

5. defy my power

They don't just go inactive. They fight against God and the Church, against all that is good, with the same energy that Satan and his evil hosts fight truth and right.

6. they are vessels of wrath

They become full of anger, bitterness, and hatred against that which is good. In other words, they actually become like Satan. They think like he does, act like he does, and react against good like he does. This is the full opposite of becoming like Christ through following His commandments and living His gospel.

7. having denied the Holy Spirit after having received it

They have received a full testimony of the gospel through the Holy Ghost, and then they intentionally lie about it and openly deny it. (See also the quote from Joseph Smith under "1. know my power" on the previous page.)

8. having denied the Only Begotten Son of the Father

Here again, one would have to possess a strong testimony of Christ and then intentionally and openly fight against Him and His work to make salvation available to all.

9. having crucified him unto themselves and put him to an open shame

They become so bitter that they would gladly crucify Christ themselves if they had the opportunity. In other words, as stated above, they have become like Satan. They think like he does, hate like he does, and have the same desires and goals as he does.

Brigham Young summarized this topic (becoming sons of perdition) as follows:

> **How much does it take** to prepare a man, or woman, . . . **to become angels to the devil, to suffer with him through all eternity?** Just as much as it does to prepare a man to go into the Celestial Kingdom,

into the presence of the Father and the Son, and to be made an heir to his kingdom and all his glory, and be crowned with crowns of glory, immortality, and eternal lives. (*Journal of Discourses* [London: Latter-day Saints' Book Depot, 1854–86] 3:93)

34

Question: Are there "daughters" of perdition?
Answer: Yes, according to Brigham Young and Melvin J. Ballard.

Brigham Young referenced women as well as men in defining what it takes to become a son of perdition. He taught,

> How much does it take to prepare **a man, or woman**, . . . to become angels to the devil, to suffer with him through all eternity? Just as much as it does to prepare a man to go into the Celestial Kingdom, into the presence of the Father and the Son, and to be made an heir to his kingdom and all his glory, and be crowned with crowns of glory, immortality, and eternal lives [*this is a description of exaltation*]. (*Journal of Discourses* [London: Latter-day Saints' Book Depot, 1854–86] 3:93)

Based on the answer to the question given above, it is obvious that the term "sons," as used in the phrase "sons of perdition," has nothing to do with gender. Rather, it means "followers of" perdition or complete followers of the devil.

Apostle Melvin J. Ballard likewise taught that women can become sons of perdition.

> He [*Heavenly Father*] has other **sons and daughters** who do not even attain unto the telestial kingdom. **They are sons of perdition**. (Bryant S. Hinckley, *Sermons and Missionary Services of Melvin J. Ballard* [Salt Lake City: Deseret Book, 1949], pp. 255–57)

35

Question: How long does the earth have between the Fall of Adam and Eve and the Final Judgment Day that follows the Millennium and the little season?
Answer: Seven thousand years.

In section 77 of the Doctrine and Covenants, Joseph Smith posed several questions dealing with the book of Revelation in the Bible, and then provided answers to those questions. One of the questions dealt with the "book" that John the Revelator (the Apostle John) saw in vision, that was in the right hand of the Father and was sealed with seven seals (Revelation 5:1). The question and answer are given in section 77 as follows:

D&C 77:6

6 Q. What are we to understand by the book which John saw, which was sealed on the back with seven seals?

A. We are to understand that it contains the revealed will, mysteries, and the works of God; the hidden things of his economy concerning **this earth** during the **seven thousand years of** its continuance, or **its temporal existence**.

This lets us know that we are getting close to the Second Coming, since we still need one thousand years for the Millennium, plus some years for the "little season" that follows, wherein Satan and his forces of evil are let loose for the final battle (D&C 88:111–14) before the Final Judgment Day. From our calendar, which is not completely accurate all the way back to Adam and Eve, we know that we have used up close to six thousand years since the Fall, which was somewhere around 4,000 BC.

36

Question: Are there people on other planets?
Answer: Yes.

Moses was given this answer when he was being oriented by the premortal Christ, or, in other words, Jehovah, preparatory for his mission to go back and lead the children of Israel out of Egyptian bondage. This vision and orientation is recorded in Moses, chapter 1, in the Pearl of Great Price. You will see the answer to this question in the heading of chapter 1 as well as in verses within this chapter.

Moses 1, chapter heading

God reveals himself to Moses—Moses transfigured—Confrontation with Satan—**Many inhabited worlds seen**—Worlds without number created by the Son—God's work and glory to bring to pass the immortality and eternal life of man.

Moses 1:31–35

31 And behold, the glory of the Lord was upon Moses, so that Moses stood in the presence of God, and talked with him face to face. And the Lord God said unto Moses: For mine own purpose have I made these things. Here is wisdom and it remaineth in me.

32 And by the word of my power, have I created them, which is mine Only Begotten Son, who is full of grace and truth.

33 And **worlds without number have I created**; and I also created them for mine own purpose; and by the Son I created them, which is mine Only Begotten.

34 And the first man of all men have I called Adam, which is many.

35 But only an account of this earth, and the inhabitants thereof, give I unto you. For behold, **there are many worlds that have passed away** by the word of my power. And **there are many that now stand**, and innumerable are they unto man; but all things are numbered unto me, for they are mine and I know them.

And so it is, that by revelation, we know for sure that there is life in outer space. They are like us, because they are all children of our Father in Heaven. And we also know, by revelation, that our Savior is also their Savior. In a series of visions, recorded in section 76 of the Doctrine and Covenants, Joseph Smith and Sidney Rigdon saw the Savior and bore witness of Him, and also that the inhabitants of other worlds created by Christ are also saved by Him. Note that the phrase "are begotten sons and daughters *unto* God" (not "of God"), in verse 24, quoted next, means "to have exaltation made available to them," or, in other words, to be "born again" through Jesus Christ in order to become exalted sons and daughters of the Father.

D&C 76:24

24 That by him [*Jesus Christ*], and through him, and of him, the worlds are and were created, and the inhabitants thereof **are begotten sons and daughters unto God**.

This is another scriptural confirmation that there are people in outer space.

37

Question: Were there really dinosaurs?
Answer: Yes.

The answer is obvious because of skeletons, footprints, and so forth found in many locations throughout the earth. Where they fit in the Creation and the Lord's plans for this earth, we do not know yet, but we will be told as part of the events that transpire with the Second Coming of Christ. This assurance comes from the Doctrine and Covenants.

D&C 101:32–34

32 Yea, verily I say unto you, in that day **when the Lord shall come, he shall reveal all things—**

33 Things which have passed, and hidden things which no man knew,

things of the earth, by which it was made, and the purpose and the end thereof—

34 Things most precious, things that are above, and things that are beneath, things that are in the earth, and upon the earth, and in heaven.

We even know that dinosaurs had spirits. Speaking of the spiritual creation (Moses 3:5), which preceded the physical creation, Apostle Bruce R. McConkie taught:

> Man and all forms of life existed as spirit beings and entities before the foundation of this earth was laid. There were spirit men and spirit beasts, spirit fowls and spirit fishes, spirit plants and spirit trees. Every creeping thing, every herb, elephant and **dinosaur**—all things—existed as spirits, as spirit beings, before they were placed naturally upon the earth. (Bruce R. McConkie, *The Millennial Messiah* [Salt Lake City: Deseret Book, 1982], pp. 642–43)

38

Question: Do all worlds have the same kind of animals?
Answer: Not necessarily.

The Prophet Joseph Smith made a comment in passing that gives us a clue that at least some of the animals on other worlds are different from those on ours. This implies that if we become gods, we will have considerable latitude as we create our own worlds and organize our ecosystems. Speaking of "beasts" seen in vision by Daniel and John the Revelator, the Prophet said,

> I suppose John saw beings there of a thousand forms, that had been saved from ten thousand times ten thousand earths like this—**strange beasts of which we have no conception**: all might be seen in heaven. (*Teachings of the Prophet Joseph Smith* [Salt Lake City: Deseret Book, 1977], p. 291)

39

Question: What's it like in the postmortal spirit world?
Answer: Wonderful in the paradise portion. A lot like here on earth in the prison portion.

We know from the scriptures that, when we die, our spirits continue life in the postmortal spirit world, which is located here on this earth (*Teachings of the Prophet Joseph Smith* [Salt Lake City: Deseret Book, 1977], p. 326, and *Discourses of Brigham Young* [Salt Lake City: Deseret Book, 1977], p. 376). There are two possible destinations in the spirit world for our spirits when we depart this life, namely, paradise or prison (Alma 40:11–14).

Paradise is a place reserved for the righteous who accepted the gospel and live it faithfully, were baptized, and will continue in their progression toward glory in the celestial kingdom. Obviously, children who die before the age of accountability also go to paradise.

Prison is the portion of the postmortal spirit world where all others go. Joseph Fielding Smith, who became the tenth President of the Church, taught this regarding the spirit world:

> As I understand it, *the righteous—meaning* **those who have been baptized and who have been faithful**—are gathered **in one part** and all **the others in another part of the spirit world**. This seems to be true from the vision given to President Joseph F. Smith and found in *Gospel Doctrine*. [*See D&C 138.*] (Joseph Fielding Smith, *Doctrines of Salvation* [Salt Lake City: Deseret Book, 1977], 2:230)

With this definition of who goes where at the time of death, it becomes obvious that there are good people as well as evil and wicked people who end up in spirit prison. Thus, it is much like our world is now. For this reason, I prefer, in most discussions, to refer to spirit prison as "the spirit world mission field." More will be said about this later. First, let's see what paradise is like.

Paradise

Apostle Bruce R. McConkie described paradise as follows:

Paradise—**the abode of righteous spirits**, as they await the day of their resurrection; paradise—**a place of peace and rest** where the sorrows and trials of his life have been shuffled off, and **where the saints continue to prepare for a celestial heaven**; paradise—not the Lord's eternal kingdom, but a way station along the course leading to eternal life, a place where the final preparation is made for that fulness of joy which comes only when body and spirit are inseparably connected in immortal glory! (Bruce R. McConkie, *The Mortal Messiah: From Bethlehem to Calvary* [Salt Lake City: Deseret Book, 1979–81], 4:222)

Brigham Young described what it is like for the righteous when they die and go to paradise.

We shall turn round and look upon it [the valley of death] and think, when we have crossed it, why this is the greatest advantage of my whole existence, for I have passed from a state of sorrow, grief, mourning, woe, misery, pain, anguish and disappointment into **a state of existence, where I can enjoy life to the fullest extent as far as that can be done without a body. My spirit is set free, I thirst no more, I want to sleep no more, I hunger no more, I tire no more, I run, I walk, I labor, I go, I come, I do this, I do that, whatever is required of me, nothing like pain or weariness, I am full of life, full of vigor, and I enjoy the presence of my heavenly Father**. (*Journal of Discourses* [London: Latter-day Saints' Book Depot, 1854–86] 17:142. See also *Doctrines of the Gospel Student Manual* [Salt Lake City: The Church of Jesus Christ of Latter-day Saints, 1986], p. 83)

Families are together in paradise but not in the prison portion of the spirit world.

Family relationships are also important. President Jedediah M. Grant, a counselor to Brigham Young, saw the spirit world and described to Heber C. Kimball the organization that exists there: "He said that the people he there saw were organized in family capacities [*in paradise*]. . . . He said, 'When I looked at families, there was a deficiency in some, . . . for I saw families that would not be permitted to come and dwell together [*in prison*], because they had not honored their calling here'" (*Deseret News*, Dec. 10, 1856, 316–17). (*Gospel Principles* [Salt Lake City: The Church of Jesus Christ of Latter-day Saints, 2009], p. 243)

Brigham Young also taught that in the spirit world, we will learn faster.

I shall not cease learning while I live, nor **when I arrive in the spirit** world; but **shall there learn with greater facility**; and when I again receive my body, I shall learn a thousand times more in a thousand times less time. (*Teachings of the Presidents of the Church: Brigham Young* [Salt Lake City: The Church of Jesus Christ of Latter-day Saints, 1997], p. 195)

Apostle Orson Pratt taught that those in paradise will not need words to communicate with each other.

For instance, how do you suppose that spirits after they leave these bodies communicate one with another? Do they communicate their ideas by the actual vibrations of the atmosphere the same as we do? I think not. I think if we could be made acquainted with the kind of language by which spirits converse with spirits, we would find that they do not communicate their ideas in this manner; they have a more refined way; I mean that portion of them that are in the school of progress; they have undoubtedly a more refined system among them of communicating their ideas. This system will be so constructed **that they can not only communicate at the same moment upon one subject**, as we have to do by making sounds in the atmosphere, **but communicate vast numbers of ideas, all at the same time, on a great variety of subjects; and the mind will be capable of perceiving them.** (Discourse of Orson Pratt, delivered in the Salt Lake Tabernacle on October 22, 1854. Printed in the *Deseret News* on December 28, 1854.)

In chapter 38 of the lesson manual for priesthood and Relief Society, *Teachings of the Presidents of the Church: Brigham Young*, we find many more details taught by President Young about what the next life will be like for those who go to paradise (Salt Lake City: The Church of Jesus Christ of Latter-day Saints, 1997).

When you are in the spirit world, **everything there will appear as natural as things now do**. Spirits will be familiar with spirits in the spirit world—will converse, behold, and exercise every variety of communication with one another as familiarly and naturally as while here in tabernacles [*as while here on earth in mortal bodies*]. There, as here, all things will be natural, and you will understand them as you now understand natural things. You will there see that **those spirits** we are speaking of **are active; they sleep not.** And you will learn that they are striving with all their might—laboring and toiling diligently as any individual would to accomplish an act in this world. (Quoted from *Discourses of Brigham Young* [Salt Lake City: Deseret Book, 1954], p. 380)

Spirits are just as familiar with spirits as bodies are with bodies, though spirits are composed of matter so refined as not to be tangible to this coarser organization. **They walk, converse, and have their meetings**; and the spirits of good men like Joseph and the Elders, who have left this Church on earth for a season to operate in another sphere, are rallying all their powers and going from place to place **preaching the Gospel**, and Joseph is directing them, saying, go ahead, my brethren, and if they hedge up your way, walk up and command them to disperse. You have the Priesthood and can disperse them, but if any of them wish to hear the Gospel, preach to them. (Ibid., p. 379)

I can say with regard to parting with our friends, and going ourselves, that I have been near enough to understand eternity so that I have had to exercise a great deal more faith to desire to live than I ever exercised in my whole life to live. **The brightness and glory of the next apartment** [*the spirit world paradise*] **is inexpressible.** It is not encumbered so that when we advance in years we have to be stubbing along and be careful lest we fall down. We see our youth, even, frequently stubbing their toes and falling down. But yonder, how different! **They move with ease and like lightning. If we want to visit Jerusalem**, or this, that, or the other place—and I presume we will be permitted if we desire—there we are, looking at its streets. If we want to behold Jerusalem as it was in the days of the Savior; or if we want to see the Garden of Eden as it was when created, **there we are**, and we see it as it existed spiritually, for it was created first spiritually and then temporally, and spiritually it still remains. And when there we may behold the earth as at the dawn of creation, or we may visit any city we please that exists upon its surface. **If we wish** to understand how they are living here on these western islands, or in China, **we are there**; in fact, we are like the light of the morning. . . . God has revealed some little things, with regard to his movements and power, and the operation and motion of the lightning furnish a fine illustration of the ability of the Almighty. (Ibid., p. 380)

When we pass into the spirit world [*paradise*] we shall possess a measure of his power. Here, we are continually troubled with ills and ailments of various kinds. **In the spirit world we are free from all this and enjoy life, glory, and intelligence;** and **we have the Father to speak to us, Jesus to speak to us, and angels to speak to us,** and **we shall enjoy the society of the just and the pure who are in the spirit world until the resurrection.** (Ibid., p. 380–81)

If we are faithful to our religion, **when we go into the spirit world** [*paradise*], **the fallen spirits—Lucifer and the third part of the heavenly hosts that came with him, and the spirits of wicked men who have dwelt upon this earth, the whole of them combined will have no influence over our spirits.** Is not that an advantage? Yes. All the rest of the children of men [*meaning those in spirit prison*] are more or less subject to them, and they are subject to them as they were while here in the flesh. (Ibid., 379)

The 2009 *Gospel Principles* manual, published by the Church, teaches more about the spirit world.

The Church is organized in the spirit world, and **priesthood holders continue their responsibilities there** (see D&C 138:30). President Wilford Woodruff taught, "**The same Priesthood exists on the other side of the veil**. . . . Every Apostle, every Seventy, every Elder, etc., who has died in the faith as soon as he passes to the other side of the veil, enters into the work of the ministry" (*Deseret News*, Jan. 25, 1882, 818). (*Gospel Principles* [Salt Lake City: The Church of Jesus Christ of Latter-day Saints, 2009], p. 243)

From the above descriptions of the paradise portion of the postmortal spirit world, we can see that life for the righteous, including children who die before the years of accountability (D&C 137:10), will be wonderful. One thing, though, that we will miss, according to the scriptures, will be our physical bodies.

In President Joseph F. Smith's vision of the Savior's visit to the postmortal spirit world (D&C 138), he saw that the righteous spirits in paradise were anxiously awaiting His visit to them after His crucifixion. Among many other things, President Smith was shown that these righteous spirits considered being without their physical bodies a difficult limitation, which they regarded as a type of bondage. They were looking forward to their resurrection, which was now imminent and would take place at the time of Christ's resurrection, only hours or days away.

D&C 138:49–50

49 All these and many more, even the prophets who dwelt among the Nephites and testified of the coming of the Son of God, mingled in the vast assembly and waited for their deliverance [*from being without physical bodies*],

50 **For the dead had looked upon the long absence of their spirits from their bodies as a bondage.**

Spirit Prison (The Spirit World Mission Field)

A brief summary of conditions in the prison portion of the postmortal spirit world is found in the 2009 edition of the *Gospel Principles* manual.

The Apostle Peter referred to the postmortal spirit world as a prison, **which it is for some** (see 1 Peter 3:18–20). **In the spirit prison are the spirits of those who have not yet received the gospel of Jesus Christ. These spirits have agency and may be enticed by both good and evil. If they accept the gospel and the ordinances performed for them in the temples, they may leave the spirit prison and dwell in paradise.**

Also in the spirit prison are those who rejected the gospel after it was preached to them either on earth or in the spirit prison. **These spirits suffer in a condition known as hell.** They have removed themselves from the mercy of Jesus Christ, who said, "Behold, I, God, have suffered these things for all, that they might not suffer if they would repent; but if they would not repent they must suffer even as I; which suffering caused myself, even God, the greatest of all, to tremble because of pain, and to bleed at every pore, and to suffer both body and spirit" (D&C 19:16–18). **After suffering for their sins, they will be allowed, through the Atonement of Jesus Christ, to inherit the lowest degree of glory, which is the telestial kingdom.** (*Gospel Principles* [Salt Lake City: The Church of Jesus Christ of Latter-day Saints, 2009], p. 244)

As mentioned above, President Joseph F. Smith received a vision in which he was shown how the dead could be redeemed. In it, he was shown how the gospel is preached to the spirits in prison. He saw that the Savior did not go personally to the spirits in prison but organized missionary work to be done among them by the righteous spirits from paradise.

D&C 138:29–31

29 And as I wondered, my eyes were opened, and my understanding quickened, and I perceived that **the Lord went not in person among the wicked and the disobedient** who had rejected the truth, to teach them;

30 But behold, **from among the righteous, he organized his forces and appointed messengers, clothed with power and authority, and commissioned them to go forth and carry the light of the gospel to them that were in darkness,** even to all the spirits of men; and thus was the gospel preached to the dead.

31 And **the chosen messengers went forth to declare the acceptable day of the Lord and proclaim liberty to the captives** [*in spirit prison*] who were bound, even unto all who would repent of their sins and receive the gospel.

Thus, the postmortal spirit prison is a vast mission field containing all but those who go to paradise (those who are faithful, baptized members of the Church and little children who die before the years of accountability). In this mission field, the devil and the evil spirits who were cast out of heaven with him (Revelation 12:4, 7–9) are free to tempt, just as here on earth. Joseph Fielding Smith, who became the tenth President of the Church, taught,

As I understand it, the righteous—meaning **those who have been baptized and who have been faithful**—are gathered **in one part** [*paradise*] and **all the others in another part of the spirit world** [*prison*]. This seems to be true from the vision given to President Joseph F. Smith. [*See D&C 138.*] (Joseph Fielding Smith, *Doctrines of Salvation* [Salt Lake City: Deseret Book, 1977], 2:230)

We see that there are good people in spirit prison and extremely wicked people in spirit prison, and every category in between, just like here on earth. Why is it called "prison"? Because all spirits in it, whether wicked or honorable and good, are limited in their progression because they do not have or have not accepted the redeeming gospel of Jesus Christ with its redeeming covenants and ordinances. Thus, they are, in effect, "behind bars" and are limited in forward progress toward heaven until if and when they accept the covenants and principles of the gospel, and when proxy ordinances are done for them in temples, which open the door to celestial glory and living with God forever.

What is taught there? Answer: the same gospel as is being taught here on earth, with the exception that spirits can't be baptized, so they are taught about proxy baptism for the dead.

D&C 138:32–35

32 **Thus was the gospel preached to those who had died** in their sins, without a knowledge of the truth, or in transgression, having reject-ed the prophets.

33 These were taught **faith** in God, **repentance** from sin, vicarious **bap-tism** for the remission of sins, the **gift of the Holy Ghost** by the laying on of hands,

34 And **all other principles of the gospel that were necessary** for them to know in order to qualify themselves that they might be judged according to men in the flesh, but live according to God in the spirit.

35 **And so it was made known among the dead**, both small and great, the unrighteous as well as the faithful, **that redemption had been wrought through the sacrifice of the Son of God upon the cross**.

The spirits who accept the gospel when they hear and understand it in the spirit prison will receive every privilege and blessing of the gospel, including exaltation, via the temple work that is done for them by mortals. President Wilford Woodruff spoke of our ancestors for whom we do the temple work. He said, "**There will be very few, if any, who will not ac-cept the gospel**." (See *Teachings of the Presidents of the Church: Wilford Woodruff* [Salt Lake City: The Church of Jesus Christ of Latter-day Saints, 2004], p. 191.)

This doctrine is comforting to those who worry about good and hon-orable loved ones and friends who have died but are not yet in paradise. They realize that these loved ones are not being punished by being sent to the spirit prison (or mission field), rather, they are being given an oppor-tunity to hear, understand, and accept the gospel, just as is the case with people on the earth. Furthermore, they must accept it in an environment of opposition and diversity of thinking and belief systems, just as we here on earth must. Once mortals do their temple work, and they accept it and are faithful there, they have every opportunity of obtaining the highest degree of glory in the celestial kingdom that we have here on earth, either here or during the Millennium. The Doctrine and Covenants is clear on this.

D&C 138:58–59

58 The dead who repent will be redeemed, through obedience to the ordinances of the house of God,

59 And after they have paid the penalty of their transgressions, and are washed clean, **shall receive a reward according to their works, for they are heirs of salvation**.

Just one more thing before we leave this topic. It sometimes bothers people that even the good people in spirit prison are called "wicked" in the scriptures. You need to know that there is more than one scriptural definition of the term "wicked."

"Wicked" is most often used in the sense of defiant, evil, intentionally breaking the commandments of God, and engaging in intentional conduct that goes against the gospel and destroys society and civilization. However, it can also mean those who do not have the gospel. This is the case in one context in the Doctrine and Covenants.

D&C 84:51–53

51 For **whoso cometh not unto me is under** the **bondage** of sin.

52 And **whoso** receiveth not my voice **is not acquainted with my voice**, and is not of me.

53 And by this you may know the righteous from the **wicked**, and that the whole world groaneth under sin and darkness even now.

Thus, the term "wicked" can simply mean those who are not yet acquainted with the gospel of Christ. There are many such good people in the postmortal spirit world, as well as here on earth. This same concept is taught in a footnote found in the *Teachings of the Prophet Joseph Smith*.

In using the term "**wicked men**,". . . the Prophet did so in the same sense in which the Lord uses it in the eighty-fourth section of the Doctrine and Covenants [*verses*] 49–53. The Lord in this scripture speaks of **those who have not received the Gospel** as being under the bondage of sin, and hence "wicked." However, **many of these people are honorable, clean living men, but they have not embraced the Gospel**. The inhabitants of the terrestrial order will remain on the earth during the Millennium, and this class are without the Gospel ordinances. (*Teachings of the Prophet Joseph Smith* [Salt Lake City: Deseret Book, 1977], pp. 268–69, fn. 2)

40

Question: Who presides in the home when the priesthood holder husband is absent?
Answer: The wife.

Elder Dallin H. Oaks addressed this topic.

When my father died, **my mother presided over our family**. She had no priesthood office, but as the surviving parent in her marriage, she had become the governing officer in her family. At the same time, she was always totally respectful of the priesthood authority of our bishop and other Church leaders. She presided over her family, but they presided over the Church.

There are many similarities and some differences in the way priesthood authority functions in the family and in the Church. If we fail to recognize and honor the differences, we encounter difficulties.

One important difference between its function in the Church and in the family is the fact that all priesthood authority *in the Church* functions under the direction of the one who holds the appropriate priesthood keys. In contrast, **the authority that presides *in the family*—whether father or single-parent mother**—functions in family matters without the need to get authorization from anyone holding priesthood keys. This family authority includes directing the activities of the family, family meetings like family home evenings, family prayer, teaching the gospel, and counseling and disciplining family members. It also includes ordained fathers giving priesthood blessings. (Dallin H. Oaks, "Priesthood Authority in the Family and the Church," October 2005 general conference)

41

Question: What is a seer?
Answer: A prophet who "sees" the past present, and future.

Seers "see" through special inspiration from God by virtue of their special callings as prophets. Because of what they "see," they can alert us to dangers that are coming that we might otherwise miss and be caught off guard by. They can also alert us about special blessings and opportunities for service to others, which will strengthen our families and us. As you know, we sustain our First Presidency and Quorum of the Twelve Apostles as "prophets, seers, and revelators." The Book of Mormon defines a seer as follows:

Mosiah 8:16–17

16 And Ammon said that **a seer is a revelator and a prophet also**; and a gift which is greater can no man have, except he should possess the power of God, which no man can; yet a man may have great power given him from God.

17 But **a seer can know of things which are past, and also of things which are to come**, and by them shall all things be revealed, or, rather, shall secret things be made manifest, and hidden things shall come to light, and things which are not known shall be made known by them, and also things shall be made known by them which otherwise could not be known.

Our prophets and seers today are vital to our spiritual survival. They "see," by special inspiration, present dangers and warn us of them. Think, for example, of some of the things they warn us about in general conferences. They see future dangers. Think of the proclamation on the family that our prophets gave us over twenty years ago on September 23, 1995, in which they warned about several coming trends and events that would work to destroy families and marriage between men and women. We are surrounded now by fulfillments of their prophetic seership and utterings.

The Prophet Joseph explained the role of seers:

Wherefore, we again say, search the revelations of God; study the prophecies, and rejoice that God grants unto the world **Seers and Prophets**. They are **they who saw** the mysteries of godliness; **they saw** the flood before it came; **they saw** angels ascending and descending upon a ladder that reached from earth to heaven; **they saw** the stone cut out of the mountain, which filled the whole earth; **they saw** the Son of God come from the regions of bliss and dwell with men on earth; **they saw** the deliverer come out of Zion, and turn away ungodliness from Jacob; **they saw** the glory of the Lord when he showed the transfiguration of the earth on the mount; **they saw** every mountain laid low and every valley exalted when the Lord was taking vengeance upon the wicked; **they saw** truth spring out of the earth, and righteousness look down from heaven in the last days, before the Lord came the second time to gather his elect; **they saw** the end of wickedness on earth, and the Sabbath of creation crowned with peace; **they saw** the end of the glorious thousand years, when Satan was loosed for a little season; **they saw** the day of judgment when all men received according to their works, and **they saw** the heaven and the earth flee away to make room for the city of God, when the righteous receive an inheritance in eternity. (*Teachings of the Prophet Joseph Smith* [Salt Lake City: Deseret Book, 1977], pp. 12–13)

42

Question: What difference does it make whether or not one serves a mission?

Answer: It can make a big difference in terms of testimony and preparation for the future.

While some are not able to serve a mission, for those who are capable and choose not to, they are missing out on a wonderful opportunity. Under the direction of the Holy Ghost, they can grow and mature tremendously in many different ways while serving. With a mission as a background, they are often far less selfish and can make good use of advanced learning and work opportunities. It has been said that when the young people who serve honorable missions return home, they, in many significant ways, are about twenty years ahead of their peers who chose not to serve.

The things mentioned above, of course, deal with personal advantages for those who choose to serve missions. Another great and significant reason for serving is the simple fact that with more people serving, there are far more of Heavenly Father's children who are brought into contact with the gospel of Jesus Christ and given the opportunity to have its stabilizing and saving influence in their lives.

43

Question: What if I'm losing myself trying to help someone else?

Answer: You may have to follow Nephi's example.

It is not uncommon for good-intentioned members of the Church to find themselves slipping spiritually, morally, or financially in their efforts to "rescue" others from their self-destructive behaviors, especially with respect to living the gospel. When this realization hits, they find themselves torn between strong feelings of obligation to save others and the fear of losing themselves. They often feel guilty, because they believe that if they were stronger in the gospel themselves, there wouldn't be a problem for their own salvation. They mistakenly believe that if they were a better person, they would be impervious to destruction when it comes to being in the unsavory environments required of them as they chaperone and watch out for those they are trying to save.

Nephi gives us the answer when it comes to such extreme situations. For many years, he had been encouraging and trying to save his brothers, Laman and Lemuel, as well as some of Ishmael's family. He was sometimes hopeful that they would change, but it never lasted. Finally, the situation was turning lethal, and Nephi was told by the Lord what to do.

<u>2 Nephi 5:1–5</u>

1 Behold, it came to pass that I, Nephi, did cry much unto the Lord my God, because of the anger of my brethren.

2 But behold, their anger did increase against me, insomuch that they did seek to take away my life.

3 Yea, they did murmur against me, saying: Our younger brother thinks to rule over us; and we have had much trial because of him; wherefore, now let us slay him, that we may not be afflicted more because of his words. For behold, we will not have him to be our ruler; for it belongs unto us, who are the elder brethren, to rule over this people.

4 Now I do not write upon these plates all the words which they murmured against me. But it sufficeth me to say, that they did seek to take away my life.

5 And it came to pass that **the Lord did warn me, that I, Nephi, should depart from them and flee** into the wilderness, and all those who would go with me.

Thus, Nephi had to stop trying to rescue them and flee for his own safety. This is sometimes the case for us when we have done all we can without success. At this point, it's time to flee the situation in order to save ourselves.

My wife once gave similar advice to a young lady whose efforts to save her friends from their own foolishness were not working. She told her, "The time has come for you to save the future mother of your own children." That statement gave her the courage and perspective to leave those peers, spend several lonely months without good friends, and finally serve a mission, marry in the temple, and have a beautiful family of her own.

44

Question: What if counsel from my bishop feels wrong?

Answer: This question requires a careful answer.

Bishops are given priesthood keys when they are set apart and ordained as a bishop. These keys include the blessings and guidance of heaven when they are giving counsel to ward members. Thus, bishops should be listened to carefully, and complying with their advice should be by far the normal course of action and thought.

But, in the rare case in which the counsel of a bishop might not be in harmony with the will of the Lord, or the member feels that this is the case, and the member is having a difficult time with conflicting feelings about following it, there is a simple path set up by the Lord to help. The path? Go see the stake president. He also has keys to counsel and help his people.

Thus, the individual member is not left without an option if he or she feels that additional counsel is necessary. Obviously, this option should not be overused, but it is good to know that the Lord is kind and has thought of everything to help us as we seek to do His will.

45

Question: What if I'm married in the temple but feel like I married the wrong person?

Answer: You could have fallen into a trap set by Satan.

Common sense tells us that there are several righteous people whom a specific person could marry and still have a life of happiness and joy with them. So, feeling that one has married the "wrong" person may not hold much credibility, and, in fact, may prove to be a dangerous deterrent to doing the necessary things that develop a strong and satisfying marriage.

Upon close examination, there may be a number of thoughtful, kind, expressions and acts that could, over time, build a marriage relationship into a growing and thriving friendship, and then, ultimately, into a desirable love affair. Some might say that this is an overly simplistic approach to a solution, but it is not. With heaven's help, such things are not only possible, but also quite common.

Let's say that yours is a rare case in which the marriage is truly not a viable match. It just isn't. Then what? Suppose you don't want to divorce for various reasons but dread being married to this person for eternity. Here are two suggestions:

One. Remember that celestial, eternal marriages, by their very nature, involve spouses who, by that time, will have become perfect, like Heavenly Father is—perfectly pleasant, perfectly nice, perfectly thoughtful, perfectly appreciative, perfectly loving, perfectly fascinating . . . well, you get the idea. Thus, it is highly likely that you will fall head over heels in love, if you haven't yet. With such an eternal mate, the prospects are very good!

Two. In the rare case where two righteous people are not eternally compatible, no worthy person will be forced against his or her will to live forever in a situation in which they are not happy. They would be allowed to remarry such that their eternal happiness would be secured. (This answer comes from personal correspondence with a representative of the First Presidency's office and then speaking for them while I was serving as a stake president.)

46

Question: Have our modern prophets and apostles seen the Savior?

Answer: It is highly likely, but it would be inappropriate to ask them.

This is a question that many of us would like to ask the Brethren, but it would be inappropriate to do so. Elder Boyd K. Packer explained this in a general conference sermon.

> Occasionally during the past year I have been asked a question. Usually it comes as a curious, almost an idle, question about the qualifications to stand as a witness for Christ. The question they ask is, "**Have you seen Him?**"
>
> **That is a question that I have never asked of another.** I have not asked that question of my brethren in the Quorum, thinking that it would be so sacred and so personal that one would have to have some special inspiration, indeed, some authorization, even to ask it.
>
> **There are some things just too sacred to discuss** . . . It is not that they are secret, but they are sacred; not to be discussed, but to be harbored and to be protected and regarded with the deepest of reverence . . . I have heard one of my brethren declare: "I know from experiences, too sacred to relate, that Jesus is the Christ."
>
> I have heard another testify: "I know that God lives; I know that the Lord lives. **And more than that, I know the Lord.**" (Excerpts from "The Spirit Beareth Record," Boyd K. Packer, April 1971 general conference)

47

Question: Why don't our prophets have real revelations like they did in ancient times?
Answer: They do.

Several years ago, one of my seminary students took her scriptures in her hand, raised them high, and sincerely asked, "Why don't our prophets nowadays have real revelations, like they used to in ancient times?" It surprised me a bit, but I complimented her for asking and assured her that it was a good question. Then, we invited the class to answer it, which they did, very nicely.

Many members, as was the case with this young student, perhaps miss the fact that our Church leaders receive ongoing revelation. These revelations are not routinely added to the books of scripture that we now carry around in our hands or on our electronic devices, but we do have access to such counsel from heaven in general conference talks, Church magazines, regional conferences, and so forth.

Think also, for example, of the word of the Lord given to the world on September 23, 1995, known as "The Family: A Proclamation to the World" from the First Presidency and Council of the Twelve Apostles of The Church of Jesus Christ of Latter-day Saints. Think also of the counsel given often by President Thomas S. Monson encouraging us to "Enjoy the journey." This revelation is badly needed by many who are caught up in the gloom and doom of the day. Consider the continuing revelations from the Lord coming directly and often through our apostles and prophets that marriage is to be only between a man and a woman. Also, think of the revelation lowering the age for missionaries to serve.

Such revelations are indeed ongoing, wonderful, and reassuring. They will continue right up to the Second Coming and beyond as Christ comes and rules as "King of kings and Lord of lords" (Revelation 19:16).

48

Question: Do animals have spirits?
Answer: Yes.

The Pearl of Great Price reveals that all things were created in spirit form before the physical creation.

Moses 3:5, 7

5 And every plant of the field before it was in the earth, and every herb of the field before it grew. For **I, the Lord God, created all things, of which I have spoken, spiritually, before they were naturally upon the face of the earth**. For I, the Lord God, had not caused it to rain upon the face of the earth. And I, the Lord God, had created all the children of men; and not yet a man to till the ground; for in heaven created I them; and there was not yet flesh upon the earth, neither in the water, neither in the air;

7 And I, the Lord God, formed man from the dust of the ground, and breathed into his nostrils the breath of life; and man became a living soul, the first flesh upon the earth, the first man also; nevertheless, **all things were before created; but spiritually were they created** and made according to my word.

Joseph Smith explained that all things have spirits and that their spirits are in the same form as their physical bodies. In section 77 of the Doctrine and Covenants, the Prophet was explaining some things found in the book of Revelation.

D&C 77:2

2 Q. What are we to understand by the four beasts, spoken of in the same verse?

A. They are figurative expressions, used by the Revelator, John, in **describing** heaven, the paradise of God, the happiness of man, and of **beasts**, and of **creeping things**, and of the **fowls** of the air; that which is spiritual being in the likeness of that which is temporal; and that which is temporal in the likeness of that which is spiritual; **the spirit of man in the likeness of his person, as also the spirit of the beast, and every other creature** which God has created.

Apostle Bruce R. McConkie said the following:

Man and all forms of life existed as spirit beings and entities before the foundation of this earth was laid. There were **spirit men and spirit beasts, spirit fowls and spirit fishes, spirit plants and spirit trees. Every creeping thing, every herb, elephant and dinosaur— all things—existed as spirits, as spirit beings, before they were placed naturally upon the earth.** (Bruce R. McConkie, *The Millennial Messiah* [Salt Lake City: Deseret Book, 1982], pp. 642–43)

49

Question: Will animals be resurrected?
Answer: Yes.

The Doctrine and Covenants is clear on this matter. Speaking of the resurrection, the Lord reveals,

<u>D&C 29:24</u> .

24 For all old things shall pass away, and **all things shall become new** [*will be resurrected*], even the heaven and the earth, and all the fulness thereof, both **men** and **beasts**, the **fowls** of the air, and the **fishes** of the sea.

50

Question: Do bugs have spirits?
Answer: Yes.

This is a revealed truth, and revelation is the only way we could possibly know the answer. The Lord revealed many things to Moses regarding the creation of this earth, including that all things were created as spirits before being created physically. This makes me happy that I belong to this true and "living" Church, meaning, among other things, that the "living God" leads it.

Moses 3:5, 7

5 I, the Lord God, created all things, of which I have spoken, spiritually, before they were naturally upon the face of the earth . . . and there was not yet flesh upon the earth, neither in the water, neither in the air; . . .

7 . . . **All things were before created; but spiritually were they created** and made according to my word.

Joseph Smith explained that all things have spirits, including "creeping things," and their spirits are in the same form as their physical bodies. In this section of the Doctrine and Covenants, the Prophet explains some things found in the book of Revelation.

D&C 77:2

2. The happiness of man, and of **beasts**, and of **creeping things**, and of the **fowls** of the air; **that which is spiritual being in the likeness of that which is temporal**; and that which is temporal in the likeness of that which is spiritual; **the spirit of man in the likeness of his person, as also the spirit of the beast, and every other creature** which God has created.

Apostle Bruce R. McConkie confirmed our understanding of this doctrine.

Man and all forms of life existed as spirit beings and entities before the foundation of this earth was laid. There were spirit men and spirit beasts, spirit fowls and spirit fishes, spirit plants and spirit trees. **Every creeping thing**, every herb, elephant, and dinosaur—all things—existed as spirits, as spirit beings, before they were placed naturally upon the earth. (*The Millennial Messiah* [Salt Lake City: Deseret Book, 1982], pp. 642–43)

51

Question: Will people besides good Mormons survive the Second Coming?
Answer: Yes.

Many residents of earth are good and honorable, honest and kind, and have high integrity. Many of them belong to various churches and strive to live their religion. Some don't belong to a church but strive to live moral and ethical lives. Some don't even believe in God because of the false and sometimes ridiculous things they have heard about Him from people who claim to be experts on the subject. Joseph Fielding Smith taught that all those whose lives reflect the standards of the terrestrial kingdom (D&C 76:71–79) or above (celestial) will not be burned at the Second Coming.

> Some members of the Church have an erroneous idea that when the millennium comes all of the people are going to be swept off the earth except righteous members of the Church. That is not so. There will be millions of people, Catholics, Protestants, agnostics, Mohammedans, people of all classes, and of all beliefs, still permitted to remain upon the face of the earth, but **they will be those who have lived clean lives, those who have been free from wickedness and corruption. All who belong, by virtue of their good lives, to the terrestrial order, as well as those who have kept the celestial law, will remain upon the face of the earth during the millennium.** (*Doctrines of Salvation* [Salt Lake City: Deseret Book, 1977], 1:86–87)

52

Question: When people who don't believe in God die, will they suddenly be converted when they find they still exist?

Answer: Not necessarily.

The Book of Mormon teaches us quite the contrary. Amulek was teaching the people not to procrastinate their repentance until it is too late when he explained that they will still be the same people when they die and enter the spirit world as they were at the close of their lives.

> Alma 34:34
>
> 34 Ye cannot say, when ye are brought to that awful crisis [*death*], that I will repent, that I will return to my God. Nay, ye cannot say this; for that same spirit which doth possess your bodies at the time that ye go out of this life, **that same spirit will have power to possess your body in that eternal world**.

The following from the *Gospel Principles* manual helps our understanding on this:

> **Spirits carry with them from earth their attitudes of devotion or antagonism toward things of righteousness** (see Alma 34:34). **They have the same appetites and desires that they had when they lived on earth.** (*Gospel Principles* [Salt Lake City: The Church of Jesus Christ of Latter-day Saints, 2009], p. 242)

53

Question: Is Christ the Savior of other worlds too or only this one?

Answer: Yes, He is the Savior for all of the Father's worlds.

Joseph Smith and Sidney Rigdon saw a powerful vision of the Savior on the right hand of the Father, as recorded in section 76 of the Doctrine and Covenants. In the course of bearing witness of Him, they gave the answer to this question.

D&C 76:24

24 That **by him, and through him, and of him, the worlds are and were created, and the inhabitants thereof are begotten sons and daughters unto God**.

As we study the words in this verse carefully, we see, in the first phrase, that the Savior is the creator of all the Father's worlds, past, present, and future. Moses was told this in his vision and interview with the Savior recorded in the Pearl of Great Price.

Moses 1:33

33 And **worlds without number have I created**; and I also created them for mine own purpose; and **by the Son I created them**, which is mine Only Begotten.

Going back to the last phrase of section 76, verse 24, quoted above, we look carefully at the word "unto" in the phrase "begotten sons and daughters unto God." Many people misread this phrase as "begotten sons and daughters of God." That's not what it says. It is "Begotten sons and daughters **unto** God." We know that we are all begotten spirit sons and daughters **of** God. In other words, we are all God's spirit children. So, what does it mean to become begotten sons and daughters "unto" God through the Savior and His gospel and Atonement? Answer: it means to have exaltation made available to us through Christ. Thus, the answer to our question is that Jesus Christ is indeed the Savior of all the Father's worlds and makes exaltation available to all of the inhabitants thereof.

However, He will not be born and raised, preach, and be crucified and resurrected repeatedly on all these worlds. Rather, His mortal life and Atonement carried out on our world will satisfy the needs for resurrection, salvation, and exaltation for the inhabitants of all the Father's other worlds. According to the parable given in D&C 88:51–61 and explained in the *Doctrine and Covenants Student Manual*, the Savior will visit other worlds for their Millenniums. (See *Doctrine and Covenants Student Manual*, Rel. 324 and 325 [Salt Lake City: The Church of Jesus Christ of Latter-day Saints, 1981], p. 201.

Just one more important revealed fact. The Book of Mormon teaches by implication that ours is the only world with wicked enough people to crucify the Savior. Jacob, Nephi's younger brother taught,

2 Nephi 10:3

3 Wherefore, as I said unto you, it must needs be expedient that Christ— for in the last night the angel spake unto me that this should be his name—should come among the Jews, **among those who are the more wicked part of the world**; and they shall crucify him—for thus it behooveth our God, and **there is none other nation on earth that would crucify their God**.

Coupled with Jacob's words, above, Enoch was told that ours is the wickedest of all God's worlds.

Moses 7:36

36 Wherefore, I can stretch forth mine hands and hold all the creations which I have made; and mine eye can pierce them also, and **among all the workmanship of mine hands there has not been so great wickedness as among thy brethren**.

As an aside comment, it is a real compliment to be sent to this earth for our mortal experience. It indicates that we are fully capable of helping the gospel go forth to fill the whole earth as prophesied.

54

Question: Why are some people healed and not others?

Answer: Life is a curriculum, so the answer varies.

This question obviously does not have just one answer. There are many variables. One important factor is God's will. He knows what is best, and we do well to trust Him. Another is "What is best for the afflicted person and those around him or her?" Since this life is indeed a "curriculum" planned by God as part of our eternal education, growth, and development, the answer will vary from person to person. One thing this mortal life is designed to develop in us is faith. If we always got our way with prayers for healing, or even administration by the priesthood for healing, we would not have to examine our faith and make sure we do not allow it to falter or fail. We all know people who were not healed, but they bore strong testimony of God and His goodness while they were still afflicted.

We see many examples in the scriptures where people have been healed. Christ healed many during His mortal ministry and after His resurrection. The Apostles also healed many during their ministry. Yet, some were not healed. For example, Paul spoke of a "thorn in the flesh" that plagued him. He had asked for healing but it didn't come. Consequently, he determined in his own mind that it must be there to keep him humble (2 Corinthians 12:7–10).

Perhaps you have noticed that sometimes a sick person is not healed because someone close to them needs to be brought closer to God through ministering to him or her. Sometimes when a faithful loved one is taken seriously ill, inactive loved ones rethink their commitment to the gospel and change their ways. Thus, the unhealed person serves as a "savior on Mount Zion" for them.

A friend of mine, who was a faithful member of the Church, was suddenly beset with a life-threatening illness. Prayers and administration did not provide healing. Her health rapidly diminished, and emergency surgery was required. She later told me that she was a bit angry with the Lord and that her last thoughts as she faded out under the effects of anesthesia were "Why me, Lord? I'm the only one in my family who is trying to live the gospel . . ."

According to what she later told me, when my friend came out of the anesthesia in the recovery room, she was still angry with God. She quickly changed her thinking, however, when she saw her inactive husband and her chain-smoking, inactive mother there at her bedside. She listened as her husband told her that he had committed to God that he would attend church with his wife every Sunday from then on if He would preserve her life. He did. I saw him in church with her every time I attended that ward in my stake.

Her mother, who was an inactive member, quietly told my friend as she recovered from the anesthesia that upon hearing of her daughter's dire circumstances, she had knelt to pray for her—with a lighted cigarette in her fingers. As she started her desperate prayer, she thought of the cigarette and the Word of Wisdom she was violating. A feeling of guilt overcame her. She stopped her prayer, put out the cigarette, and went through her house gathering every pack and carton of cigarettes she had stashed away. She took them all out and deposited them in the trash. She returned to her prayer, apologized for her violation of the Word of Wisdom, covenanted to never smoke again, and then, with a clear conscience, asked God to heal her daughter.

Upon discovering what her illness had done in bringing her family closer to the Lord, my friend told me that she ceased her complaining and, instead, thanked her Father in Heaven that she could serve them in such a manner.

55

Question: Is God increasing in knowledge?
Answer: No.

Some people theorize and philosophize on this topic and come up with the answer that He has to be growing or increasing in knowledge in His own realm. Otherwise, He would get bored. They are wrong. They fall into the sad intellectual category described by Paul:

2 Timothy 3:7

7 **Ever learning, and never able to come to the knowledge of the truth.**

The Book of Mormon answers this question.

2 Nephi 9:20

20 O how great the holiness of our God! For **he knoweth all things, and there is not anything save he knows it**.

The Institute of Religion's *Book of Mormon Student Manual* gives two quotes, one from *Lectures on Faith*, and one from Elder Neal A. Maxwell of the Quorum of the Twelve. Be aware that the word "omniscient" used in these quotes means "all knowing."

First quote

The Lectures on Faith teach why **the omniscience of God is necessary**: "Without the **knowledge of all things** God would not be able to save any portion of his creatures; for it is by reason of the knowledge which he has of all things, from the beginning to the end, that enables him to give that understanding to his creatures by which they are made partakers of eternal life; and if it were not for the idea existing in the minds of men that God had all knowledge it would be impossible for them to exercise faith in him" ([1985], 51–52). (*Book of Mormon Student Manual* [Salt Lake City: The Church of Jesus Christ of Latter-day Saints, 2009], p. 67)

Second Quote

Elder Neal A. Maxwell explained that God must know all things in order to accomplish His work of bringing to pass our immortality and eternal life.

> Those who try to qualify **God's omniscience** fail to understand that He has no need to avoid ennui [*tedium*] by learning new things. Because God's love is also perfect, there is, in fact, divine delight in that "one eternal round" which, to us, seems to be all routine and repetition. **God derives His great and continuing joy and glory by increasing and advancing His creations, and not from new intellectual experiences.**
>
> **There is a vast difference, therefore, between an omniscient God and the false notion that God is on some sort of post-doctoral fellowship, still searching for additional key truths and vital data.** Were the latter so, God might, at any moment, discover some new truth not previously known to Him that would restructure, diminish, or undercut certain truths previously known by Him. Prophecy would be mere prediction. Planning assumptions pertaining to our redemption would need to be revised. Fortunately for us, however, His plan of salvation is constantly underway—not constantly under revision. . . .
>
> In a very real sense, all we need to know is that **God knows all!** (*All These Things Shall Give Thee Experience* [Salt Lake City: Deseret Book, 1979], 14–15, 21). (*Book of Mormon Student Manual* [Salt Lake City: The Church of Jesus Christ of Latter-day Saints, 2009], p. 67)

56

Question: Is my child, who died at age three, a little orphan in the spirit world?

Answer: No.

A member of my ward asked me this question while I was serving as bishop. She understood this to be the case and, by the time she asked the question, had lived under a sense of great sadness at the thought for several years. The correct answer took a great burden from her soul and replaced it with joy. The following quote from *Gospel Principles* explains that there are no children in the postmortal spirit world. They are all adult spirits.

> **All spirits are in adult form.** They were adults before their mortal existence, and they are in adult form after death, even if they die as infants or children (see *Teachings of Presidents of the Church: Joseph F. Smith* [Salt Lake: The Church of Jesus Christ of Latter-day Saints, 1998], p. 131–32). (Quoted in *Gospel Principles* [Salt Lake City: The Church of Jesus Christ of Latter-day Saints, 2009], p. 242)

57

Question: I have heard that if I am worthy, I will be able, during the Millennium, to raise my little child who died. Is this true?
Answer: Yes.

President Joseph F. Smith recounted what the Prophet Joseph Smith taught on this subject.

> Joseph Smith declared that **the mother who laid down her little child**, being deprived of the privilege, the joy, and the satisfaction of bringing it up to manhood or womanhood in this world, would, after the resurrection [*which takes place for the righteous at the beginning of the Millennium*], have all the **joy, satisfaction and pleasure**, and even more than it would have been possible to have had in mortality, **in seeing her child grow to the full measure of the stature of its spirit.**
>
> **When the mother is deprived of the pleasure and joy of rearing her babe to manhood or to womanhood in this life, through the hand of death, that privilege will be renewed to her hereafter**, and she will enjoy it to a fuller fruition than it would be possible for her to do here. When she does it there, it will be with the certain knowledge that the results will be without fail. (*Gospel Doctrine* [Salt Lake City: Deseret Book, 1977], p. 453–54)

Joseph Fielding Smith reminds us that this privilege of raising little children after the resurrection at the beginning of the Millennium is for parents who are worthy of exaltation, or, in other words, for fathers and mothers together, not just mothers alone.

If parents are righteous, they will have their children after the resurrection. Little children who die, whose parents are not worthy of exaltation, will be adopted into the families of those who are worthy. (*Doctrines of Salvation* [Salt Lake City: Deseret Book, 1977], 2:56)

58

Question: If I am worthy, will I be able to be with my stillborn child in the next life?
Answer: Yes.

The Encyclopedia of Mormonism helps answer this question.

Although temple ordinances are not performed for stillborn children, **no loss of eternal blessings or family unity is implied**. The family may record the name of a stillborn child on the family group record followed by the word *stillborn* in parentheses. (*The Encyclopedia of Mormonism* [New York: Macmillan, 1992]; see "Stillborn")

Apostle Bruce R. McConkie gave the following reassurance:

The spirit enters the body at the time of quickening, months prior to the actual normal birth. The value and comfort attending a knowledge of this eternal truth is seen in connection with stillborn children. Since the spirit entered the body before birth, **stillborn children will be resurrected and righteous parents shall enjoy their association in immortal glory**. (*Doctrinal New Testament Commentary* [Salt Lake City: Bookcraft, 1977], 1:84–85)

59

Question: What about aborted babies?

Answer: We have no revealed doctrine yet on this.

Over the years, a few faithful and wonderful mothers have shared personal, sacred experiences with me as their bishop, stake president, or teacher in which assurances were given them that their babies, lost through spontaneous abortions, would belong to them in the next life.

On the other hand, a mother who had lost a baby to spontaneous abortion tearfully shared her testimony with me that the next child born to her and her husband was the spirit of her baby lost through abortion. I have no problem believing both scenarios, since a merciful God is in charge. However, such personal witnesses should not become the basis for proclaiming Church doctrine. Thus, we must wait for further official word from the Lord on this subject.

60

Question: I understand that the Constitution will "hang by a thread." Will it be saved?

Answer: Yes.

In our day, it seems that we are watching the Constitution of the United States of America being unraveled. It is not that the actual wording of the Constitution is being changed. Rather, lawmakers and the courts of our land are reinterpreting the intent and meaning of the founding fathers, thus rendering their inspired purpose and wording ineffective. The Lord makes it clear that He established the Constitution of the United States of America by the hands of the founding fathers. These were wise and inspired men who were sent to earth and positioned by the Lord for this exact purpose.

<u>D&C 101:77–80</u>

77 According to **the laws and constitution** of the people, **which I have suffered to be established**, and should be maintained for the rights and protection of all flesh, according to just and holy principles;

78 **That every man may act** in doctrine and principle pertaining to futurity, **according to** the **moral agency** which I have given unto him, **that every man may be accountable for his own sins** in the day of judgment.

79 Therefore, it is not right that any man should be in bondage one to another.

80 And for this purpose have **I established the Constitution of this land, by the hands of wise men whom I raised up unto this very purpose**, and redeemed the land by the shedding of blood.

Brigham Young was one of a number who prophesied that the day would come that the Constitution would hang by a thread. He also said that it would not be destroyed but would be saved by members of the Church. We will include two statements from Brigham Young here.

Will the Constitution be destroyed? No.

It will be held inviolate by this people; and, as Joseph Smith said, "The time will come when the destiny of the nation will hang upon a single thread. **At that critical juncture, this people will step forth and save it from the threatened destruction.**" It will be so. (*Journal of Discourses* [London: Latter-day Saints' Book Depot, 1854–86], 7:15)

When the Constitution of the United States hangs, as it were, upon a single thread, they will have to call for the "Mormon" elders to save it from utter destruction; **and they will step forth and do it**. (Ibid., 2:182)

President Ezra Taft Benson also prophesied of this. He taught,

Unfortunately, we as a nation have apostatized in various degrees from different Constitutional principles as proclaimed by the inspired founders. **We are fast approaching that moment prophesied by Joseph Smith** when he said: "Even this nation will be on the very verge of crumbling to pieces and tumbling to the ground, and **when the Constitution is upon the brink of ruin, this people will be the staff upon which the nation shall lean, and they shall bear the Constitution away from the very verge of destruction**" (19 July 1840, as recorded by Martha Jane Knowlton Coray; manuscript in Church Historian's Office, Salt Lake City). (Quoted in President Ezra Taft Benson's "Our Divine Constitution," *Ensign,* November 1987.)

For me, one of the values in knowing that these prophets have assured us that the Constitution will be saved is that I don't have to watch in total despair as the Constitution is assaulted. Rather, I can watch with confident curiosity (not complacency) to see how it will be saved. Of course, we must all strive to the best of our ability and circumstance to help save it.

61

Question: What if I can't forgive someone?
Answer: Turn it over to the Savior.

In some extreme circumstances, it can be seemingly impossible to forgive. Often, the most difficult cases are when someone has hurt a loved one. In other words, it is often easier to forgive someone who has caused you extreme trauma than someone who has severely abused or distressed a family member or someone else you love.

The Savior gave us the key for these and all situations in which forgiving seems difficult or even beyond our capability. It is found in verse 11 of the following verses.

D&C 64:9–11

9 Wherefore, I say unto you, that ye ought to forgive one another; for he that forgiveth not his brother his trespasses standeth condemned before the Lord; for there remaineth in him the greater sin.

10 I, the Lord, will forgive whom I will forgive, but of you it is required to forgive all men.

11 And **ye ought to say in your hearts—let God judge between me and thee**, and reward thee according to thy deeds.

Thus, the Savior invites us to turn such a situation over to Him and let Him handle it. This, in turn, frees us from the great damage done to our soul by harboring judgment and hatred and desires for revenge. Such feelings, usually intended to damage the person or persons responsible for our hurt, instead place us in the very real emotional "prison" spoken of in scripture.

Matthew 5:25–26

25 Agree [*make peace, work things out*] with thine adversary quickly, whiles thou art in the way with him; lest at any time the adversary deliver thee to the judge, and the judge deliver thee to the officer, **and thou be cast into prison**.

26 Verily I say unto thee, **Thou shalt by no means come out thence, till thou hast paid the uttermost farthing**.

Sometimes we may not want to turn it over to the Savior, because we want the satisfaction of hating, despising, being angry, wishing bad things on the perpetrator, and so forth. Perhaps the first step in such situations would be to pray sincerely for God to soften our heart to the point that we will turn it over to Him. When we get to the point prayed for, we can do it and are set free. We feel a great burden lifted, and life begins to be beautiful.

One misconception that can cause additional pain is to think that "forgiving" means to continue putting up with abuse. It does not. Nephi had to "flee" his abusive brothers (2 Nephi 5:5). This can be an important example to others.

The important thing is to be willing to turn the perpetrator over to the Savior for Him to deal with. This gives the victim who is struggling a "time out," so to speak, for things to settle down and for him or her to gradually gain the strength to forgive.

In summary, one of the first steps toward healing is to pray that you can get to the point where you are able to say, in effect, "I will turn it over to the Savior and simply and honestly support what He does with, to, or for the perpetrator."

62

Question: Can a perpetrator of child sexual abuse be forgiven?
Answer: Yes.

This sin usually leads to excommunication. It may take several years of deep and sincere repentance before the First Presidency or Twelve grant permission for a person guilty of sexually abusing a child to be rebaptized. However, it can be done. I saw it while serving as a stake president. When all the requirements are accomplished, the person guilty of so vile a sin comes forth out of the waters of baptism pure and clean, with a new and bright future before him or her. It is a reminder of the tremendous and beautiful power of the Atonement of Christ to cleanse and heal.

63

Question: What if the child he or she sexually abused can't get over it? Is forgiveness still available to the perpetrator?
Answer: Yes.

Personal forgiveness is not dependent upon the behaviors of other people. For example, if someone we have wronged refuses to forgive us, even after we have sincerely and repeatedly begged for forgiveness, made restitution as much as possible, pled for forgiveness from the Lord, and so forth, we can be forgiven and made clean, pure, and fit to return into the presence of God. Such is the power of the Atonement of Jesus Christ. The sin of denying the Holy Ghost (Alma 39:5) is the only sin for which forgiveness is not available. Even first degree, intentional murder for selfish purposes can be forgiven to the degree of at least entering the telestial kingdom (D&C 76:103; Revelation 22:15). Most murderers do not have a full knowledge of the gospel, so their accountability is less, which means they can completely be forgiven through repentance.

64

Question: Will victims of abuse ever be healed and have a decent chance?

Answer: Yes.

Many victims of abuse are able, with counseling and other help, to successfully put the past behind them and move ahead to build a satisfying and successful life with the gospel and the Savior as their foundation and central focus. However, it seems that some are not able to recover to this point during the rest of their mortal lives. What about them?

The answer: God is completely fair. Such individuals will be healed in the next life and enabled to progress toward eternal happiness, marriage, and exaltation in their own family units, if they so choose. The Bible confirms with beautiful words that they will be healed.

Revelation 21:4

4 And **God shall wipe away all tears from their eyes**; and there shall be no more death, **neither sorrow, nor crying, neither shall there be any more pain: for the former things are passed away**.

The Doctrine and Covenants teaches that those whose lives are damaged by the behavior of others will be "reclaimed."

D&C 50:7

7 Behold, verily I say unto you, there are hypocrites among you, who have deceived **some**, which has given the adversary power; but behold **such shall be reclaimed**.

65

Question: I thought I was inspired to marry my spouse. What happened?

Answer: This could be fraught with danger or, on rare occasions, could be a valid concern.

This question itself implies that a marriage isn't going well. There are several possible general answers. One is that you were inspired to marry your spouse, and it could have worked out well, but your spouse, over time, has exercised agency to change attitudes about you and the marriage.

Another possibility is that it could have worked out well, but you have exercised your agency and have now changed your feelings about your spouse and the marriage.

In either case, you would both be well advised to humbly consider what attracted you to each other in the first place. Prayerfully and openly discuss inspired solutions that could rekindle attraction and love. In so doing, you will most likely be able to rebuild your marriage and once again discover what you originally saw in each other. It would obviously require time, work, and unselfishness, but the results could be wonderful!

Another possible answer is that you were not inspired. Rather, you mistook your feelings or the advice of others at that time as inspiration and missed or avoided promptings that warned you not to marry your spouse. There are, no doubt, myriad scenarios that could have led up to the current dilemma you now face regarding your marriage. So, what now?

First of all, before you make any final decisions, make sure your own life is in order so you can receive and recognize inspiration. It is critical that you receive and follow it now. With the help of the Holy Ghost, you can avoid making a major mistake. Many marriages are not only saved but are also significantly enhanced when the simple basics of charity, kindness, civility, pleasant communication, valid compliments, and other courtesies are emphasized in daily living. Often, these simple virtues are the things that get pushed aside in the rush of daily life.

And finally, you are not alone. You have a bishop and a stake president, both of whom have had keys conferred upon them by which they are authorized to provide you with inspired counsel and direction. Many marriages are energized and saved by using these resources provided by the Lord.

66

Question: What if I'm not happy in my temple marriage?

Answer: Prayerfully and humbly analyze the situation and see what you might do to bring more happiness into the marriage.

This answer assumes that both you and your spouse are currently striving to be faithful and active in the Church. Otherwise, you might want to read the answer to the previous question.

One major thing that honorable and faithful people in this situation often fail to consider is that in the distant future, both they and their spouse will become gods. As such, they will then be married to a perfect being—perfectly pleasant, perfectly nice, perfectly fascinating, kind, loving, intelligent, interesting, responsible—and the list goes on. All of the character traits and attributes that attracted you to the marriage in the first place will be perfected, and all the bothersome and difficult personality imper-fections that have crept into or persisted in the marriage, that have now reached the point of making the marriage less than desirable, will be gone. Remember that *your* annoying traits will also be gone!

In summary, as you and your spouse progress toward becoming gods, you will simultaneously approach perfection in loving each other. The things in your marriage that are now troubling you will gradually be over-come, and they will be replaced by a love that you now cannot imagine! This perspective may be helpful to you at present. It can inspire you toward being more patient, thoughtful, and loving in your daily relationship with your spouse, insomuch that your marriage will even now begin to grow more pleasant and satisfying.

67

Question: What if I'm worthy but never find someone to marry in the temple during this life?

Answer: You will be blessed to find someone and marry during the Millennium.

This is one of the most comforting of doctrines and a reminder of the fair-ness of God to all His children. A quote from *True to the Faith* verifies this doctrine.

> **Some members of the Church remain single through no fault of their own, even though they want to marry.** If you find yourself in this situation, be assured that "all things work together for good to them that love God" (Romans 8:28). **As you remain worthy, you will someday, in this life or the next, be given all the blessings of an eternal fami-ly relationship.** The Lord has made this promise repeatedly through His latter-day prophets.
>
> If you are single and desire to be married, do not give up hope. At the same time, **do not allow yourself to become preoccupied with your**

goal. **Instead, become anxiously engaged in worthwhile activities.** Look for ways to serve in your extended family and in your community. Accept and magnify Church callings. Keep yourself clean, both physically and spiritually. **Continue to learn and develop and progress in your personal life.** (*True to the Faith* [Salt Lake City: The Church of Jesus Christ of Latter-day Saints, 2004], p. 99)

If it turns out to be in the next life for you personally, here is one possible scenario. After you die, you will meet and grow in love with someone who is worthy in the postmortal spirit world. In the course of your courting, you will agree to marry. But since you are spirits, and mortals must perform ordinances for the dead (D&C 128:15 and 18), your marriage will be performed for you by proxy during the Millennium. Thus, you are not left out, and you and your spouse will go on to receive and enjoy all the blessings of family and exaltation.

68

Question: Is military killing murder?
Answer: No.

Consider righteous Captain Moroni in the Book of Mormon. He and his noble soldiers, including Helaman's 2060 stripling warriors (Alma 56–57), were forced to defend their people because of attacks by their enemies. As we read about these wars, beginning with Alma, chapter 43, in the Book of Mormon, we see a lot of military killing in defense of the people of God. Yet, these men remained righteous in the eyes of God. We see this in Mormon's description of Captain Moroni and others involved in this conflict.

Alma 48:16–18

16 And also, that God would make it known unto them whither they should go to defend themselves against their enemies, and by so doing, the Lord would deliver them; and **this was the faith of Moroni, and his heart did glory in it; not in the shedding of blood but in doing good, in preserving his people,** yea, in keeping the commandments of God, yea, and resisting iniquity.

17 Yea, verily, verily I say unto you, **if all men had been, and were, and ever would be, like unto Moroni, behold, the very powers of hell would have been shaken forever**; yea, the devil would never have power over the hearts of the children of men.

18 Behold, **he was a man like unto Ammon, the son of Mosiah, yea, and even the other sons of Mosiah, yea, and also Alma and his sons, for they were all men of God.**

69

Question: Is it true that if an angel appears to you, you should ask him to shake hands?
Answer: This is context sensitive.

The Prophet Joseph Smith gave the counsel to invite a messenger appearing to you to shake hands. This instruction came during a time in the early days of the Restored Church when it was somewhat common for Satan and his evil spirits to attempt to deceive members by appearing as angels from God and delivering false messages. You can read about this in the heading to section 50 of the Doctrine and Covenants. The Prophet's counsel on this subject is found in section 129. In it, he explains that three possible types of beings can appear to you: (1) angels (resurrected beings) sent from God, (2) righteous spirits sent from God, and (3) evil spirits pretending to be angels of light. The instruction in the verses below is simple and straightforward.

D&C 129:4–8

4 When a messenger comes saying he has a message from God, **offer him your hand and request him to shake hands with you.**

5 **If he be an angel he will do so, and you will feel his hand.**

6 **If he be the spirit of a just man made perfect** [*a righteous spirit who is not yet resurrected*] **he will come in his glory; for that is the only way** he can appear—

7 **Ask him to shake hands with you, but he will not move, because it is contrary to the order of heaven for a just man to deceive**; but he will still deliver his message.

8 **If it be the devil as an angel of light, when you ask him to shake hands he will offer you his hand, and you will not feel anything; you may therefore detect him**.

This instruction can obviously be beneficial today under certain circumstances, but for members who are sensitive to the Spirit, they would recognize true messengers from God by the gift of the Holy Ghost, and by the same means, they would recognize an evil spirit attempting to deceive. Thus, under most circumstances, spiritually mature members would probably not need to ask to shake hands unless they were inspired to do so by the Holy Ghost.

70

Question: What are the most commonly mentioned gifts of the Spirit?
Answer: The ones mentioned in D&C 46:13–25, 1 Corinthians 12:5–10, and Moroni 10:9–16.

Here are the gifts of the Spirit most commonly referred to in talks and discussions.

D&C 46:13–25

13 To some it is given by the Holy Ghost **to know that Jesus Christ is the Son of God**, and that he was crucified for the sins of the world.

14 To others it is given **to believe on their words**, that they also might have eternal life if they continue faithful.

15 And again, to some it is given by the Holy Ghost **to know the differences of administration**, as it will be pleasing unto the same Lord, according as the Lord will, suiting his mercies according to the conditions of the children of men.

16 And again, it is given by the Holy Ghost to some **to know the diversities of operations**, whether they be of God, that the manifestations of the Spirit may be given to every man to profit withal.

17 And again, verily I say unto you, to some is given, by the Spirit of God, the word of **wisdom**.

18 To another is given the word of **knowledge**, that all may be taught to be wise and to have knowledge.

19 And again, to some it is given to have **faith to be healed**;

20 And to others it is given to have **faith to heal**.

21 And again, to some is given **the working of miracles**;

22 And to others it is given to **prophesy**;

23 And to others **the discerning of spirits**.

24 And again, it is given to some **to speak with tongues**;

25 And to another is given **the interpretation of tongues**.

1 Corinthians 12:5–10

5 And there are **differences of administrations**, but the same Lord.

6 And there are **diversities of operations**, but it is the same God which worketh all in all.

7 But the manifestation of the Spirit is given to every man to profit withal.

8 For to one is given by the Spirit the word of **wisdom**; to another the word of **knowledge** by the same Spirit;

9 To another **faith** by the same Spirit; to another the **gifts of healing** by the same Spirit;

10 To another the **working of miracles**; to another **prophecy**; to another **discerning of spirits**; to another *divers* kinds of **tongues**; to another the **interpretation of tongues**:

Moroni 10:9–16

9 For behold, to one is given by the Spirit of God, that he may teach the word of **wisdom**;

10 And to another, that he may teach the word of **knowledge** by the same Spirit;

11 And to another, exceedingly great **faith**; and to another, the **gifts of healing** by the same Spirit;

12 And again, to another, that he may **work mighty miracles**;

13 And again, to another, that he may **prophesy concerning all things**;

14 And again, to another, the **beholding of angels and ministering spirits**;

15 And again, to another, all kinds of **tongues**;

16 And again, to another, the **interpretation of languages and of divers kinds of tongues**.

Perhaps you noticed that Moroni 10:14 mentions one gift that none of the other references mention. It is the "beholding of angels and ministering spirits," or, in other words, seeing angels and righteous spirits.

Doctrine and Covenants 46:13 informs us that the Holy Ghost gives us these gifts of the Spirit. We will provide a brief description of each of the gifts mentioned in the above verses.

1. **The gift of knowing that Jesus is the Christ**. In other words, to have a sure witness by the power of the Holy Ghost that Jesus is indeed the Christ, the Son of the living God.

2. **The gift of believing the testimony of those who do know**. In other words, to have a testimony from the Spirit that enables you to believe strongly the words of those who do have a sure witness that the gospel is true. Such belief gives these members the strength to live the gospel faithfully, and for many, it keeps them on the strait and narrow path until they receive their own sure testimony. For others, it keeps them on the path until they enter heaven and find out for sure for themselves.

3. **To know the differences of administration**. This gift includes the skill of leadership and includes understanding how best to use the

Church organization. This is especially noticeable in the Prophet, General Authorities, general auxiliary leaders, stake presidents, bishops, and local quorum and auxiliary leaders. An example might be to have the ability to quickly decide in a ward council meeting which auxiliary organization or priesthood group or quorum to assign to best carry out a ward service project or activity.

4. **The diversity of operations**. The gift of distinguishing between false philosophies of men and truths from God—good ideas and bad ideas, wise counsel and foolish counsel, and whether something is from God or another source. For example, sometimes we might not be able to discern what is wrong with something we are hearing or that is being taught to us, but this gift warns us not to trust it. Often, with further study, or even later on in life, we come to understand what was wrong in that situation and are greatly relieved that we had this gift to prevent us from succumbing to false teachings or invitations to follow a different path.

5. **The gift of wisdom**. You've no doubt met some who are endowed with extra wisdom and common sense. Those with this gift of the Spirit are of great value to others and society as a whole. Once in a while, someone reads the wording of this gift, which, in the scriptures, reads, "the word of wisdom," and mistakenly interprets it to mean no tea, coffee, alcohol, or tobacco, as given in section 89 of the Doctrine and Covenants. Such is not the case.

6. **The gift of knowledge.** Some are given the gift of acquiring and retaining knowledge. Often, the gift of teaching goes along with this gift.

7. **The gift of faith to be healed.** Some are blessed with the gift of being able to pray in faith and be healed more frequently than might be considered usual, or, in other words, they have the gift of being healed when administered to by priesthood holders.

8. **The gift of faith to heal.** This gift applies to physical as well as spiritual healings. In an eternal perspective, being healed spiritually

or of bitterness and anger, gaining a testimony, being converted to the Church, and many other such things are no doubt even more important than physical healing.

A bit of caution needs to go along with the discussion of this gift. Those who have this gift are sometimes called upon to the point that they become the unofficial "designated blessers and healers" in a given ward or locality. As a result, those who would normally be called upon to administer to the sick, such as fathers, brothers, home teachers, and so forth, are excluded from consideration. This is, of course, not an absolute rule, but wisdom should prevail.

By the way, the gift of healing is not limited to priesthood holders. Faithful women, including mothers, are often blessed with this gift and use it through their prayers of faith in behalf of their sick. The Prophet Joseph Smith spoke of faithful sisters healing the sick. He said, "If the sisters should have faith to heal the sick, let all hold their tongues, and let everything roll on" (*Teachings of the Prophet Joseph Smith* [Salt Lake City: Deseret Book, 1977], p. 224).

9. **The gift of the working of miracles.** Here, as with the gift of healing, we may tend to think of the spectacular. If we do so, we may miss the "working of miracles" that abounds on a less obvious level. For example, the miracle of lessening contention, the impression to call someone, the sudden inspiration to solve a problem, the impression leading to avoiding a traffic accident, the impression to speak a kind word rather than a scathing rebuke. The list is endless.

10. **The gift of prophecy.** In John 16:13, we are taught that the Holy Ghost "shall shew you things to come." Therefore, we understand that, among other things, this gift (which all members can have, and which must be kept within proper stewardship and realm of influence) can include the gift of knowing the future. Certainly, the First Presidency and the members of the Quorum of the Twelve have this gift for their stewardship over the entire world. We sustain

them as "prophets, seers, and revelators." Other leaders within the Church can have this gift for those within their stewardships. Parents can have it for their families.

As a personal example, I was working late on a Saturday evening studying and making notes for a talk I was to give on the following day. However, my mind kept focusing on the fact that one of our daughters was not yet home and it was getting late. Suddenly, I was given to know that she would be driving in within the next few minutes. With this peace of mind, I was able to concentrate on preparing the talk. Sure enough, within ten minutes, I heard the unmistakable sound of our Ford pickup in the driveway. She was home. The gift of prophecy had provided comfort before the fact.

A faithful member could have the gift of prophesy by way of a good feeling or an uncomfortable feeling when dealing with a decision affecting the future. The gift of prophecy could be helpful in choosing a career path in college, choosing between employment options, deciding whether to relocate, deciding what discipline would be best for a child, and so forth.

11. **The gift of discerning of spirits.** This gift helps us sense good or evil in others. For example, sometimes we can walk into a room where others are gathered and sense a pleasant, calm spirit and atmosphere. On the other hand, we might enter a crowd of people and strongly feel evil and potential damage to our soul. Another aspect of this gift is the ability to see the good in others. In Conference Report, April 1950, page 162, Elder Stephen L. Richards explained that in addition to sensing hidden evil or good, this gift also enables one who possesses it to see the good in others.

12. **The gift of tongues.** This is the gift of speaking other languages or hearing a foreign language and understanding it. This gift was manifested on the day of Pentecost when Peter and the Apostles spoke to the multitude in their own language, and those in the crowd understood the words of the Apostles in their own tongue (Acts 2:4–13).

Perhaps the most common manifestation of this gift in our day is found in the comparatively rapid rate at which our missionaries called to foreign-language missions learn to speak their respective languages. Joseph Smith cautioned us about the use of this gift, because it is often counterfeited by the devil as a means of deceiving people. The Prophet Joseph Smith taught, "Be not so curious about tongues, do not speak in tongues except there be an interpreter present; the ultimate design of tongues is to speak to foreigners, and if persons are very anxious to display their intelligence, let them speak to such in their own tongues. The gifts of God are all useful in their place, but when they are applied to that which God does not intend, they prove an injury, a snare and a curse instead of a blessing" (*History of the Church*, [Salt Lake City: The Church of Jesus Christ of Latter-day Saints, 1932–51], 5:31–32).

13. **The gift of the interpretation of tongues.** This gift usually appears in conjunction with the gift of tongues. Elder Bruce R. McConkie taught, "Tongues and their interpretation are classed among the signs and miracles which always attend the faithful and which stand as evidences of the divinity of the Lord's work (Mormon 9:24, Mark 16:17, and Acts 10:46). In their more dramatic manifestations, they consist in speaking or interpreting, by the power of the Spirit, a tongue which is completely unknown to the speaker or interpreter. Sometimes it is the pure Adamic language which is involved" (*Doctrinal New Testament Commentary*, [Salt Lake City: Bookcraft, 1970], 2:383).

This gift, as is the case with the gift of tongues, is most often found in the work of spreading the gospel to all the earth. Certainly, those who work with translating the scriptures and Church curriculum materials into foreign languages for use as the Church spreads forth into all nations would experience this gift.

14. **The gift of the beholding of angels and ministering spirits** (mentioned in Moroni 10:14). This is the gift of being able to see angels and spirits. When those who have this gift are prompted to share with us what they see or have seen, it strengthens our testimonies.

71

Question: Are there other gifts of the Spirit?
Answer: Yes.

The Lord teaches that there are indeed many gifts of the Spirit.

D&C 46:11

11 For all have not every gift given unto them; for **there are many gifts**, and to every man is given a gift by the Spirit of God.

Elder Marvin J. Ashton, of the Quorum of the Twelve, mentioned a number of these other gifts of the Spirit in a general conference talk several years ago.

Let us review some of these less-conspicuous gifts: the gift of **asking**; the gift of **listening**; the gift of **hearing and using a still, small voice**; the gift of **being able to weep**; the gift of **avoiding contention**; the gift of **being agreeable**; the gift of **avoiding vain repetition**; the gift of **seeking that which is righteous**; the gift of **not passing judgment**; the gift of **looking to God for guidance**; the gift of **being a disciple**; the gift of **caring for others**; the gift of **being able to ponder**; the gift of **offering prayer**; the gift of **bearing a mighty testimony**; and the gift of **receiving the Holy Ghost**. ("There Are Many Gifts," Marvin J. Ashton, in Conference Report, October 1987)

The Apostle Paul also mentioned a number of these other gifts.

Romans 12:6–13

6 Having then gifts differing according to the grace that is given to us, whether prophecy [*if we have **the gift of prophecy**]*, let us prophesy according to the proportion of faith [*according to how much faith we have*];

7 Or ministry [*if we have **the gift of serving others**]*, let us wait on [*attend to*] our ministering [*let us serve others*]: or he that teacheth [*he who has **the gift of teaching**]*, on teaching [*let him teach*];

8 Or he that exhorteth [*he who has* **the gift of preaching and encouraging others to do right**], on exhortation: he that giveth [*he who has* **the gift of generosity**], let him do it with simplicity [*without drawing much attention to himself*]; he that ruleth [*has* **the gift of leadership**], with diligence [*let him be diligent in leading and fulfilling his duties*]; he that sheweth mercy [*he who has* **the gift of being merciful**], with cheerfulness [*let him use it cheerfully*].

9 Let love be without dissimulation [*let* **the gift of love** *be used sincerely, without hypocrisy*]. Abhor that which is evil [**the gift of shunning evil**]; cleave to that which is good [**the gift of deeply desiring to be involved with good**].

10 Be kindly affectioned [**the gift of being friendly**] one to another with brotherly love; in honour preferring one another [**the gift of leading by good example and honor**];

11 Not slothful in business [**the gift of being skilled in business**]; fervent in spirit [**the gift of spirituality**]; serving the Lord [**the gift of being naturally faithful to God**];

12 Rejoicing in hope [**the gift of having hope and confidence**, *which comes through living Christ's gospel*]; patient in tribulation [**the gift of having patience during trials and troubles**]; continuing instant in prayer [**the gift of being in constant communication with God**];

13 Distributing [**the gift of sharing**] to the necessity of saints [*sharing according to the needs of the Saints*]; given to hospitality [**the gift of hospitality**].

72

Question: What does "steadying the ark" mean?
Answer:　　Telling Church leaders how to run the Church.

This phrase comes from section 85, verse 8, of the Doctrine and Covenants. It is a warning to Bishop Edward Partridge who, at the time, was refusing to issue deeds (as instructed in D&C 51:4) to the Saints for property they had been allocated. He was pushing back against the Brethren and, in effect, telling them how to run the Church.

The original "steadying the ark" incident comes from the Old Testament. In 2 Samuel 6:6–7, a man named Uzzah, against strict warnings that no one other than authorized priests should touch the Ark of the Covenant, stretched forth his hand to steady it when he thought it was going to fall off its cart as it was being pulled by oxen. He was struck dead as a result.

73

Question: How accountable are intellectually handicapped people?

Answer: Generally speaking, they are in the same category as little children before the years of accountability.

This answer is found in the Doctrine and Covenants.

D&C 29:50

50 And **he that hath no understanding, it remaineth in me to do according as it is written**. And now I declare no more unto you at this time. Amen.

The words in bold, above, require a bit of explanation in order to derive this answer. "He that hath no understanding" includes babies, young children, and most intellectually handicapped individuals. Many intellectually handicapped people function in a range similar to that of young children. "According as it is written," at the time of this revelation, would refer to Moroni, chapter 8, in the Book of Mormon. In this chapter, Mormon writes to Moroni regarding the abominable practice of baptizing little children. He states that "little children are whole, for they are not capable of committing sin" (Moroni 8:8). Furthermore, "And their little children need no repentance, neither baptism" (Moroni 8:11). And, finally, "Little children are alive in Christ" (Moroni 8:12). In other words, little children are saved through Jesus Christ. Thus, the intellectually handicapped, who have "no understanding," and who are like "little children," are likewise "alive in Christ."

This answer is further substantiated elsewhere in the Doctrine and Covenants.

D&C 29:46–47

46 But behold, I say unto you, that **little children are redeemed from the foundation of the world through mine Only Begotten**;

47 Wherefore, **they cannot sin, for power is not given unto Satan to tempt little children, until they begin to become accountable before me**.

D&C 68:27

27 And their **children shall be baptized for the remission of their sins when eight years old**, and receive the laying on of the hands.

D&C 137:10

10 And I also beheld that **all children who die before they arrive at the years of accountability are saved in the celestial kingdom of heaven**.

Since the intellectually handicapped, to whom we are referring, never "arrive at the years of accountability" during this life, we know that they "are saved in the celestial kingdom of heaven."

74

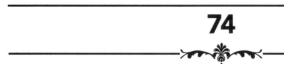

Question: What are intelligences?
Answer: We don't know.

Joseph Fielding Smith, who became the tenth President of the Church, explained this as follows:

The intelligent part of man was not created but always existed. There has been some speculation and articles have been written attempting to explain just what these "**intelligences**" are, or this "**intelligence**" is, but **it is futile for us to speculate upon it**. We do know that intelligence was not created or made and cannot be, because the Lord has said it [*D&C 93:29*]. There are some truths it is well to leave until the Lord sees fit to reveal the fulness. (*Church History and Modern Revelation* [Salt Lake City: Deseret Book, 1947], 1:401. See also the Institute of Religion's *Doctrines of the Gospel Student Manual*, Rel. 430 and 431 [Salt Lake City: The Church of Jesus Christ of Latter-day Saints, 2004], p. 13.)

75

Question: Can sons of perdition be forgiven?
Answer: No.

The Doctrine and Covenants clearly states this.

D&C 76:32–34

32 They are they who are the **sons of perdition**, of whom I say that it had been better for them never to have been born;

33 For they are vessels of wrath, doomed to suffer the wrath of God, with the devil and his angels in eternity;

34 **Concerning whom I have said there is no forgiveness in this world nor in the world to come—**

76

Question: How is the next prophet selected?
Answer: It is an automatic process set up by the Lord.

When the President of the Church dies, succession is automatic. A quote from *Teachings of the Living Prophets* confirms this.

> **Succession in the prophetic office is automatic and proceeds according to apostolic seniority in the Quorum of the Twelve**. . . . The leadership change is automatic and instantaneous. A special revelation is not necessary. (*Teachings of the Living Prophets* [Salt Lake City: The Church of Jesus Christ of Latter-day Saints, 1982], p. 32)

Thus, the Lord has already put things in place by His choice of who has now been an Apostle the longest. For example, when President Joseph Fielding Smith died and Harold B. Lee was called as our prophet, Spencer W. Kimball, President Lee's successor, explained the process of succession as follows:

> **Full provision has been made by our Lord for changes**. Today there are fourteen apostles holding the keys in suspension, the twelve and the two counselors to the President, to be brought into use if and when circumstances allow, all ordained to leadership in their turn as they move forward in seniority. There have been some eighty apostles so endowed since Joseph Smith, though only eleven have occupied the place of the President of the Church, death having intervened; and since the death of his servants is in the power and control of the Lord, **he permits to come to the first place only the one who is destined to take that leadership**. Death and life become the controlling factors. Each new apostle in turn is chosen by the Lord and revealed to the then living prophet who ordains him. The matter of seniority is basic in the first quorums of the Church. All the apostles understand this perfectly, and all well-trained members of the Church are conversant with this perfect succession program. ("We Thank Thee, O God, for a Prophet," in Conference Report, Oct. 1972, p. 29; or *Ensign*, Jan. 1973, p. 34)

77

Question: Is it true that the Prophet can't lead us astray?

Answer: Yes.

The Lord makes this clear in the Doctrine and Covenants. Early on, He explained the pattern whereby we can know that the Prophet would not be allowed to lead the Church astray.

D&C 35:17–18

17 And **I have sent forth the fulness of my gospel by the hand of my servant Joseph**; and in weakness have I blessed him;

18 And **I have given unto him the keys** of the mystery of those things which have been sealed, even things which were from the foundation of the world, and the things which shall come from this time until the time of my coming, **if he abide in me** [*if he remains true to his calling as the Prophet*], **and if not, another will I plant in his stead** [*if not, I will remove him and place another in the calling as the Prophet*].

This pattern is repeated by the Lord a bit later in the Doctrine and Covenants.

D&C 43:3–6

3 And this ye shall know assuredly—that **there is none other appointed unto you to receive commandments and revelations** until he be taken, **if he abide in me** [*if the Prophet follows God's instructions*].

4 But verily, verily, I say unto you, that **none else shall be appointed unto this gift except it be through him**; for **if it be taken from him** [*if he tries to lead the Church astray*] **he shall not have power except to appoint another in his stead** [*he would only have power to appoint a successor*].

5 And **this shall be a law unto you**, that ye receive not the teachings of any that shall come before you as revelations or commandments;

6 And **this I give unto you that you may not be deceived**, that you may know they [*any who accuse the Prophet of attempting to lead the Church astray*] are not of me.

Those who claim that the Church is off track would do well to pay close attention to this ironclad promise from the Lord Himself.

78

Question: How do I "receive" the Holy Ghost?
Answer: It requires effort and awareness on your part.

The word "receive" implies action. Therefore, "receiving" the Holy Ghost requires action and obedience on the part of members of the Church who have been confirmed by the laying on of hands and instructed to "receive the Holy Ghost" by a Melchizedek Priesthood holder. We read the following from the Church, published in *True to the Faith* (bold added for emphasis):

> Full enjoyment of the gift of the Holy Ghost includes receiving revelation and comfort, serving and blessing others through spiritual gifts, and being sanctified from sin and made fit for exaltation in the celestial kingdom. These blessings depend on your worthiness; they come a little at a time as you are ready for them. **As you bring your life in harmony with God's will, you gradually receive the Holy Ghost in great measure**. The Prophet Joseph Smith declared that the mysteries of God's kingdom "are only to be seen and understood by the power of the Holy Spirit, which God bestows on those who love him, and purify themselves before him" (see D&C 76:114–16).

> Remember that "the Spirit of the Lord doth not dwell in unholy temples" (Helaman 4:24**). Even though you have received the gift of the Holy Ghost, the Spirit will dwell with you only when you keep the commandments. He will withdraw if you offend Him by profanity, uncleanliness, disobedience, rebellion, or other sins. Keep yourself clean. Fill your life with goodness so you can be worthy of the constant companionship of the Holy Ghost**. (*True to the Faith* [Salt Lake City: The Church of Jesus Christ of Latter-day Saints, 2004], pp. 83–84)

79

Question: **What if I don't seem able to get much out of the endowment session?**

Answer: **It can be helpful to focus on what it really is.**

Perhaps you need to adjust your approach to it and focus more on what it really is. For example, the temple is Heavenly Father's classroom, and His inspired curriculum (the endowment) in this classroom is designed to teach you His plan for helping you return successfully to His presence. Be aware that He uses symbolism in His teaching, including the clothing worn during the endowment. Also, be aware that it is His way of walking you through the plan of salvation, all the way from premortality to when you symbolically enter His presence at the end of the endowment. He instructs you in what you need to do and the attitudes you need to develop. He provides covenants for you to keep that will protect you, and instructs you about things to avoid. In time, you will come to understand that your agency and covenants play a vital role in helping you succeed in gaining exaltation in His presence forever. They also help you avoid the wiles of Satan, whose goals include distracting you from the gospel and making you miserable.

As mentioned above, even the special clothing worn during the endowment (which you can see online at lds.org) involves symbolism. You might find it helpful to read Exodus 28, where it describes special clothing worn by the priests while officiating in the Aaronic Priesthood sacrifices and rites associated with the tabernacle and the law of Moses. As you do so, you will become more aware that the clothing we wear during the endowment is similar to that worn during sacred rites in ancient times. While serving as a stake president, I made it a point to alert my people who were receiving their endowment for the first time that the temple clothing might make them feel like they were stepping back into Old Testament times. Some of the sacred clothing is mentioned in Exodus 28:4, 42.

<u>Exodus 28:4, 42</u>

4 And these *are* the garments which they shall make; a breastplate, and an **ephod** [*an apron*], and a **robe**, and a broidered coat, a **mitre** [*a cap*], and a **girdle** [*a sash*]: and they shall make holy garments for Aaron thy brother, and his sons, that he may minister unto me in the priest's office.

42 And thou shalt make them **linen breeches** [*undergarments or* under-pants] **to cover their nakedness**; from the loins even unto the thighs they shall reach.

In conclusion, we will mention two items of clothing that have symbolic meaning in some cultures, ancient and modern, that can have relevance to our temple worship today.

Veil over the face—worn to show reverence and respect before God and in the presence of important people (Genesis 24:65).

Caps or hats—worn to show reverence and respect before God. For example, the skullcap or "kippah," worn by many Jewish men and boys, symbolizes their awareness of and submission to God. The practice has its roots in biblical times when priests in the tabernacle and temple were required to cover their heads.

80

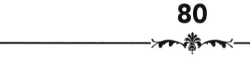

Question: Why do bad things happen to good people?
Answer: This is easier to comprehend and accept if we understand that God designed our mortal lives for our growth and development.

You will notice from your reading of the scriptures that all kinds of "bad things" happen to good people. According to Lehi, it is, of necessity, part of the plan.

<u>2 Nephi 2:11</u>

11 For **it must needs be, that there is an opposition in all things**. If not so, my first–born in the wilderness, righteousness could not be brought to pass, neither wickedness, neither holiness nor misery, neither good nor bad. Wherefore, all things must needs be a compound in one; wherefore, if it should be one body it must needs remain as dead, having no life neither death, nor corruption nor incorruption, happiness nor misery, neither sense nor insensibility.

God does not promise that if we keep His commandments we will be kept free of trials and tribulations. Rather, He promises that we will be supported during them. Joseph Smith learned this lesson.

<u>D&C 3:8</u>

8 Yet you should have been faithful; and he would have extended his arm and **supported you against all the fiery darts of the adversary; and he would have been with you in every time of trouble**.

Sometimes the trials and difficulties we go through help those around us. For example, an older sister in one of my classes fell suddenly ill with a life-threatening infection. She later told me that just before going under the anesthesia in preparation for emergency surgery, she was angry with God for letting it happen to her, especially since she was one of the few members of her family who were active in the Church.

In the recovery room, her first thoughts as she regained consciousness were that she was still angry with God. Then she saw her inactive mother and husband by her bedside. They both told her that they had pled with God to spare her life, and that if He did, they would return to Church. They kept their word. Her anger turned to gratitude that her suffering could be the means of bringing about blessings to her loved ones.

81

Question: How do you get a temple divorce?
Answer: December 1975 *New Era* article

Elder James A. Cullimore answered this question in response to a question submitted to the *New Era* magazine.

> As to the first question, "What happens when a couple gets a temple divorce?" we should understand that **there is no such thing as a temple divorce**. What we refer to as a temple divorce is in fact **a cancellation of a temple sealing**. When a couple is married in the temple, they not only satisfy the law of the land as to a legal civil marriage, but they are also sealed for time and all eternity in an eternal relationship. (Elder James A. Cullimore, "Questions and Answers," *New Era*, December 1975)

Elder Cullimore went on to explain that a request for cancellation of sealing must be submitted to the First Presidency.

> A civil divorce nullifies the marriage so far as the civil law is concerned, but **only by a mandate of the President of the Church can the sealing of the couple be canceled**. A cancellation of the sealing is what we are really referring to when we talk about a temple divorce. (Ibid.)

When a couple seeks a cancellation of their temple sealing, they work through their bishop, who has the required forms for submitting a request for cancellation of sealing to the First Presidency.

82

Question: Who were some of the angels who taught Joseph Smith?
Answer: President John Taylor mentioned several.

The following quotes from some of President Taylor's talks help us realize how many personages were involved. Some names are repeated in different talks.

> When God selected Joseph Smith to open up the last dispensation . . . **the Father** and **the Son** appeared to him . . . **Moroni** came to Joseph . . . Then comes another personage, whose name is **John the Baptist** . . . Afterwards came **Peter**, **James** and **John** . . . Then we read again of **Elias** or **Elijah** . . . who committed to him the powers and authority associated with his position. Then **Abraham**, who had the Gospel, the Priesthood and Patriarchal powers in his day; and **Moses** who stood at the head of the gathering dispensation in his day . . . We are informed that **Noah**, who was a Patriarch, and **all in the line of the Priesthood, in every generation back to Adam**, who was the first man, possessed the same. Why was it that all these people . . . could communicate with Joseph Smith? Because he stood at the head of the dispensation of the fullness of times . . . If you were to ask Joseph what sort of a looking man Adam was, he would tell you at once; he would tell you his size and appearance and all about him. You might have asked him what sort of men Peter, James and John were, and he could have told you. Why? Because he had seen them. (*Journal of Discourses* [London: Latter-day Saints' Book Depot, 1854–86], 18: 325–26)

> And when Joseph Smith was raised up as a Prophet of God, **Mormon, Moroni, Nephi**, and **others of the ancient Prophets who formerly lived on this Continent**, and **Peter** and **John** and **others who lived on the Asiatic Continent**, came to him and communicated to him certain principles pertaining to the gospel of the Son of God. (Ibid., 17:374)

> I know of what I speak for I was very well acquainted with him [*Joseph Smith*] and was with him a great deal during his life, and was with him

when he died. The principles which he had, placed him in communication with the Lord, and not only with the Lord, but with the ancient apostles and prophets, such men, for instance, as **Abraham, Isaac, Jacob, Noah, Adam, Seth, Enoch,** and **Jesus** and **the Father,** and **the apostles that lived on this continent as well as those who lived on the Asiatic Continent.** He seemed to be as familiar with these people as we are with one another. (Ibid., 21:94)

83

Question: Is it true that Joseph came to get Emma when she died?

Answer: Yes.

From an article in the *Ensign* magazine, we read the following:

Emma lived almost thirty-five years after the martyrdom of her Prophet-husband. She died 30 April 1879 in her seventy-fifth year. In her last years she was greatly loved, and in the last hours of her life she was attended by her family: Louis Bidamon, Julia, Joseph III, and Alexander. According to Alexander, Emma seemed to sink away, but then she raised up and stretched out her hand, calling, **"Joseph! Joseph!"** Falling back on Alexander's arm, she clasped her hands on her bosom, and her spirit was gone. Both Alexander and Joseph thought she was calling for her son Joseph, but later, Alexander learned more about the incident. Sister Elizabeth Revel, Emma's nurse, explained that **a few days earlier Emma had told her that Joseph came to her in a vision** and said, **"Emma, come with me, it is time for you to come with me."** As Emma related it, she said, "I put on my bonnet and my shawl and went with him; I did not think that it was anything unusual. I went with him into a mansion, and he showed me through the different apartments of that beautiful mansion." And one room was the nursery. In that nursery was a babe in the cradle. She said, "I knew my babe, my Don Carlos that was taken from me." She sprang forward, caught the child up in her arms, and wept with joy over the child. When Emma recovered herself sufficient she turned to Joseph and said, "Joseph, where are the rest of my children?" He said to her, "Emma, be patient and you shall have all of your children." Then **she saw standing by his side a personage of**

light, even the Lord Jesus Christ. (Gracia N. Jones, "My Great-Great-Grandmother, Emma Hale Smith," *Ensign*, August 1992)

84

Question: Was there gender in premortality?
Answer: Yes.

In "The Family: A Proclamation to the World" we read the answer.

> All human beings—male and female—are created in the image of God. Each is a beloved spirit son or daughter of heavenly parents, and, as such, each has a divine nature and destiny. **Gender is an essential characteristic of individual premortal, mortal, and eternal identity and purpose.** ("The Family: A Proclamation to the World," September 23, 1995; see also *Ensign*, November 1995)

This pure doctrine, revealed truth directly from the Lord through the First Presidency and the Council of the Twelve Apostles, given on September 23, 1995, is vital for members to understand in our day of great confusion and conflicting statements and philosophies regarding gender.

85

Question: How many versions of the First Vision are there?

Answer: We currently have four by Joseph Smith and five secondhand accounts by his contemporaries who heard him talk about it.

You can read these accounts on the Church's website, lds.org. (Search for "accounts of the First Vision.") A brief summary of the four known primary accounts found on lds.org is given here.

1832 Account. The earliest known account of the First Vision, the only account written in Joseph Smith's own hand, is found in a short, un-published autobiography Joseph Smith produced in the second half of 1832. In the account, Joseph Smith described his consciousness of his own sins and his frustration at being unable to find a church that matched the one he had read about in the New Testament and that would lead him to redemption. He emphasized Jesus Christ's Atone-ment and the personal redemption it offered. He wrote that "the Lord" appeared and forgave him of his sins. As a result of the vision, Joseph experienced joy and love, but as he noted, he could find no one who believed his account.

1835 Account. In the fall of 1835, Joseph Smith recounted his First Vision to Robert Matthews, a visitor to Kirtland, Ohio. The retelling, recorded in Joseph's journal by his scribe Warren Parrish, emphasizes his attempt to discover which church was right, the opposition he felt as he prayed, and the appearance of one divine personage who was followed shortly by another. This account also notes the appearance of angels in the vision.

1838 Account. The narration of the First Vision best known to Latter-day Saints today is the 1838 account. First published in 1842 in the *Times and Seasons,* the Church's newspaper in Nauvoo, Illinois, the account was part of a longer history dictated by Joseph Smith between peri-ods of intense opposition. Whereas the 1832 account emphasizes the more personal story of Joseph Smith as a young man seeking forgive-ness, the 1838 account focuses on the vision as the beginning of the "rise and progress of the Church." Like the 1835 account, the central question of the narrative is which church is right.

1842 Account. Written in response to *Chicago Democrat* editor John Wentworth's request for information about the Latter-day Saints, this account was printed in the *Times and Seasons* in 1842. (The "Went-worth Letter," as it is commonly known, is also the source for the Ar-ticles of Faith.) The account, intended for publication to an audience unfamiliar with Mormon beliefs, is concise and straightforward. As with earlier accounts, Joseph Smith noted the confusion he experienced and the appearance of two personages in answer to his prayer. The following year, Joseph Smith sent this account with minor modifications to a historian named Israel Daniel Rupp, who published it as a chapter in his book *He Pasa Ekklesia* [The Whole Church]: *An Original History of the Religious Denominations at Present Existing in the United States.*

The five secondhand accounts are as follows. (You can read them on lds.org.)

1. **Orson Pratt, A[n] Interesting Account, pp. 3–5.** This is the earliest published account of Joseph Smith's first vision of Deity. It was written by Orson Pratt of the Quorum of the Twelve Apostles and published as a pamphlet in Scotland in 1840.

2. **Orson Hyde, Ein Ruf aus der Wüste [A cry out of the wilderness], pp. 14–16** (original German) (modern English translation). Another member of the Quorum of the Twelve, Orson Hyde, published this account of Joseph Smith's earliest visions in Frankfurt, Germany, in 1842.

3. **Levi Richards, Journal, 11 June 1843.** Following an 11 June 1843 public church meeting at which Joseph Smith spoke of his earliest vision, Levi Richards included an account of it in his diary.

4. **Interview, JS by David Nye White, Nauvoo, IL, 21 Aug. 1843**; in David Nye White, "The Prairies, Joe Smith, the Temple, the Mormons, &c.," *Pittsburgh Weekly Gazette,* 15 Sept. 1843, [3]. In August 1843, David Nye White, editor of the *Pittsburgh Weekly Gazette,* interviewed Joseph Smith in his home as part of a two-day stop in Nauvoo, Illinois. His news article included an account of Joseph Smith's first vision.

5. **Alexander Neibaur, Journal, 24 May 1844.** On 24 May 1844, German immigrant and Church member Alexander Neibaur visited Joseph Smith in his home and heard him relate the circumstances of his earliest visionary experience.

86

Question: Will Christ ever become a Heavenly Father and have His own worlds?

Answer: Yes.

The answer to this question is found in the Doctrine and Covenants. It is just a brief statement of doctrinal fact but serves to answer this question.

D&C 76:106–8

106 These are they who are cast down to hell and suffer the wrath of Almighty God, until the fulness of times, **when Christ shall have subdued all enemies under his feet, and shall have perfected his work**;

107 **When he shall deliver up the kingdom, and present it unto the Father**, spotless, saying: I have overcome and have trodden the wine-press alone, even the wine-press of the fierceness of the wrath of Almighty God.

108 **Then shall he be crowned with the crown of his glory, to sit on the throne of his power to reign forever and ever.**

87

Question: Will the Holy Ghost ever get a body?

Answer: Yes.

We find this answer in a statement by Joseph Smith quoted in the *Ensign.*

The Bible gives little detail about the personage of the Holy Ghost. The Prophet, however, gave us a number of insights about that spirit being and his office. On several occasions, especially in Nauvoo in 1842–43, the Prophet spoke of the Holy Ghost as a being "in the form of a personage," as a "spirit without tabernacle," separate and distinct from the personages of the Father and the Son. According to the George Laub journal, on another occasion Joseph taught that "**the Holy Ghost is** yet a spiritual body and **waiting to take to himself a body**." ("The Restoration of Major Doctrines through Joseph Smith: The Godhead, Mankind, and the Creation," *Ensign*, January 1989, p. 29)

88

Question: When did we get agency?
Answer: We know for sure that we were given agency as premortal spirits.

The scriptures teach that we were given agency in premortality. Here are two passages of scripture dealing with the war in heaven.

D&C 29:36

36 And it came to pass that Adam, being tempted of the devil—for, behold, the devil was before Adam, for he rebelled against me, saying, Give me thine honor, which is my power; and also **a third part of the hosts of heaven turned he away from me because of their agency**.

Moses 4:1–3

1 AND I, the Lord God, spake unto Moses, saying: That Satan, whom thou hast commanded in the name of mine Only Begotten, is the same which was from the beginning, and he came before me, saying—Behold, here am I, send me, I will be thy son, and I will redeem all mankind, that one soul shall not be lost, and surely I will do it; wherefore give me thine honor.

2 But, behold, my Beloved Son, which was my Beloved and Chosen from the beginning, said unto me—Father, thy will be done, and the glory be thine forever.

3 Wherefore, because that **Satan** rebelled against me, and **sought to destroy the agency of man, which I, the Lord God, had given him**, and also, that I should give unto him mine own power; by the power of mine Only Begotten, I caused that he should be cast down.

We know that we were taught the gospel in our premortal life and could use our agency there to make choices whether or not to obey God's commandments. We could sin and repent there. An Institute of Religion's student manual used by the Church says the following:

We were given laws and agency, and commandments to have faith and repent from the wrongs that we could do there. "Man could and did in many instances, sin before he was born" (Joseph Fielding Smith, *The Way to Perfection* [Salt Lake City: Deseret Book, 1975], p. 44). (Quoted in *The Life and Teachings of Jesus and His Apostles*, Rel. 211 and 212 [Salt Lake City: The Church of Jesus Christ of Latter-day Saints, 1979], p. 336)

89

Question: How long will people live during the Millennium?
Answer: They will live to age one hundred.

Isaiah gave us this answer. Speaking of the Millennium, he taught,

Isaiah 65:20

20 There shall be no more thence an infant of days, nor an old man that hath not filled his days: for the child shall die **an hundred years old**; but the sinner *being* **an hundred years old** shall be accursed.

Additional quotes substantiate this answer.

In the Millennium children will grow up and live upon the earth until they are **one hundred years old.** (See Isaiah 65:20; D&C 101:29–31; 63:50–51; 45:58.) **Men shall die when they are one hundred years of age,** and the change shall be made suddenly to the immortal state (Joseph Fielding Smith, *The Way to Perfection* [Salt Lake City: Deseret Book, 1975], pp. 298–99). (*Doctrines of the Gospel Student Manual,* Rel. 430 and 431 [Salt Lake City: The Church of Jesus Christ of Latter-day Saints, 2004], p. 103–4)

90

Question: Is it true that there was a cave in the Hill Cumorah with lots of Nephite records?

Answer: Yes.

Brigham Young spoke of this at a special conference in Farmington, Utah, held to organize a new stake, on June 17, 1877.

> I believe I will take the liberty to tell you of another circumstance that will be as marvelous as anything can be. This is an incident in the life of Oliver Cowdery, but he did not take the liberty of telling such things in meeting as I take. I tell these things to you, and I have a motive for doing so. I want to carry them to the ears of my brethren and sisters, and to the children also, that they may grow to an understanding of some things that seem to be entirely hidden from the human family. Oliver Cowdery went with the Prophet Joseph when he deposited these plates. Joseph did not translate all of the plates; there was a portion of them sealed, which you can learn from the Book of Doctrine and Covenants. When Joseph got the plates, the angel instructed him to carry them back to the hill Cumorah, which he did. **Oliver says that when Joseph and Oliver went there, the hill opened, and they walked into a cave**, in which there was a large and spacious room. He says he did not think, at the time, whether they had the light of the sun or artificial light; but that it was just as light as day. They laid the plates on a table; it was a large table that stood in the room. **Under this table there was a pile of plates** as much as two feet high, and **there were altogether in this room more plates than probably many wagon loads**; they were piled up in the corners and along the walls. The first time they went there the sword of Laban hung upon the wall; but when they went again it had been taken down and laid upon the table across the gold plates; it was unsheathed, and on it was written these words: "This sword will never be sheathed again until the kingdoms of this world become the kingdom of our God and his Christ." I tell you this as coming not only from Oliver Cowdery, but others who were familiar with it. (*Journal of Discourses* [London: Latter-day Saints' Book Depot, 1854–86], 19:38)

91

Question: The Doctrine and Covenants says that after faithful elders die, they preach in the spirit world. How about faithful women?

Answer: Faithful sisters also preach there after they die.

President Joseph F. Smith had a vision of the missionary work going on in the postmortal spirit world. In it, he saw faithful elders who had died and gone to paradise preaching the gospel in the prison portion of the spirit world.

D&C 138:57

57 **I beheld that the faithful elders** of this dispensation, **when they depart from mortal life, continue their labors in the preaching of the gospel** of repentance and redemption, through the sacrifice of the Only Begotten Son of God, **among those who are in darkness and under the bondage of sin in the great world of the spirits of the dead**.

President Joseph F. Smith taught also that faithful sisters from this world, after they die, will indeed help preach the gospel in the spirit world.

These good **sisters . . . will be fully authorized and empowered to preach the gospel and minister to the women while the elders and prophets are preaching it to the men**. The things we experience here are typical of the things of God and the life beyond us. (*Gospel Doctrine* [Salt Lake City: Deseret Book, 1977], p. 461)

92

Question: What is the success rate of temple work we do for our ancestors?

Answer: Very high.

President Wilford Woodruff provided the answer to this question.

> Many of our progenitors, now in the spirit world, never saw the face of an apostle, prophet or inspired man, and they are shut up in prison. Joseph Smith, Heber Kimball, George A. Smith and thousands of the elders of Israel may preach to those spirits, and they may receive the testimonies which the elders bear; but the elders will not baptize believers there; there is no baptism in the spirit world any more than there is any marrying and giving in marriage . . . Our forefathers are looking to us to attend to this work. They are watching over us with great anxiety, and are desirous that we should finish these temples and attend to certain ordinances for them, so that in the morning of the resurrection they can come forth and enjoy the same blessings that we enjoy . . . So it will be with your fathers. **There will be very few, if any, who will not accept the Gospel** . . . The fathers [*ancestors*] of this people will embrace the Gospel. (*Teachings of the Presidents of the Church: Wilford Woodruff*, "Temple Work: Becoming Saviors on Mount Zion" [Salt Lake City: The Church of Jesus Christ of Latter-day Saints, 2004], 18:184–94)

93

Question: How do little children who die get married?
Answer: During the Millennium, by proxy.

They will choose a mate in the spirit world or during the Millennium. Then they will introduce themselves and their fiancé to mortals during the Millennium who will be sealed for them by proxy in a temple. Joseph Fielding Smith taught this. He said,

We have people coming to us all the time just as fearful as they can be that a child of theirs who has died will lose the blessings of the kingdom of God unless that child is sealed to someone who is dead. They do not know the wishes of their child who died too young to think of marriage, but they want to go straight to the temple and have a sealing performed. Such a thing as this is unnecessary and in my judgment wrong.

The Lord has said through his servants that **during the millennium those who have passed beyond and have attained the resurrection will reveal in person to those who are still in mortality all the information which is required to complete the work of these who have passed from this life. Then the dead will have the privilege of making known the things they desire and are entitled to receive**. In this way, no soul will be neglected and the work of the Lord will be perfected. (*Doctrines of Salvation* [Salt Lake City: Bookcraft, 1956], 3:65)

94

Question: What is the source of instinct in animals?
Answer: The Light of Christ.

Parley P. Pratt, an early Apostle in the Restored Church, taught this. Speaking of the "Light of Christ" (D&C 88:7), he explained,

This light manifests itself in different ways and degrees. In its "less refined existence," wrote Parley P. Pratt, "it is visible as sunlight. It is also the refined intellectual light of our inward and spiritual organs, by which we reason, discern, judge, compare, comprehend, and remember the subjects within our reach." **It is revealed as instinct in animals**, reason in man, and vision in the prophets. (*The Encyclopedia of Mormonism* [New York: Macmillan, 1992]; see "Light of Christ")

95

Question: Are little children who die before the years of accountability just saved in the celestial kingdom, or do they receive exaltation?

Answer: They receive exaltation.

This is one of the beautiful revealed truths of the gospel. First of all, Joseph Smith was shown in a vision that they are saved in the celestial kingdom.

<u>D&C 137:10</u>

10 And I also beheld that **all children who die before they arrive at the years of accountability are saved in the celestial kingdom of heaven**.

We understand that the phrase "years of accountability" means age eight, which is the earliest age at which children can be baptized.

<u>D&C 68:25–27</u>

25 And again, inasmuch as parents have children in Zion, or in any of her stakes which are organized, that teach them not to understand the doctrine of repentance, faith in Christ the Son of the living God, and of baptism and the gift of the Holy Ghost by the laying on of the hands, **when eight years old**, the sin be upon the heads of the parents.

26 For this shall be a law unto the inhabitants of Zion, or in any of her stakes which are organized.

27 And **their children shall be baptized for the remission of their sins when eight years old**, and receive the laying on of the hands.

Furthermore, President Joseph F. Smith taught that they will receive exaltation, which is the highest degree of glory in the celestial kingdom.

Under these circumstances, our beloved friends who are now deprived of their little one, have great cause for joy and rejoicing, even in the midst of the deep sorrow that they feel at the loss of their little one for a time.

155

They know he is all right; they have the assurance that their little one has passed away without sin. Such children are in the bosom of the Father. **They will inherit their glory and their exaltation**, and they will not be deprived of the blessings that belong to them; for, in the economy of heaven, and in the wisdom of the Father, who doeth all things well, those who are cut down as little children are without any responsibility for their taking off, they, themselves, not having the intelligence and wisdom to take care of themselves and to understand the laws of life; and, in the wisdom and mercy and economy of God our Heavenly Father, all that could have been obtained and enjoyed by them if they had been permitted to live in the flesh will be provided for them hereafter. **They will lose nothing by being taken away from us in this way**. (*Gospel Doctrine* [Salt Lake City: Deseret Book, 1977], pp. 452–53)

This brings up the question, "How can they receive exaltation since they did not have a temple marriage?" The answer is simple. As adults in the next life, they will be able to date, court, and grow in love. Then, during the Millennium, they will introduce themselves to mortal members of the Church and ask them to be sealed for them by proxy in a temple. They will thus finish qualifying for exaltation.

96

Question: Do we really have a Mother in Heaven?
Answer: Yes.

In the proclamation on the family, the First Presidency and Quorum of the Twelve Apostles clearly teach that we have Heavenly Parents. Thus, we have a Mother in Heaven as well as a Father in Heaven.

All human beings—male and female—are created in the image of God. Each is a beloved spirit son or daughter of **heavenly parents**, and, as such, each has a divine nature and destiny. ("The Family: A Proclamation to the World," September 23, 1995; see also *Ensign*, November 1995)

While speaking to Latter-day Saint young women during an area conference in Mexico City, President Spencer W. Kimball taught,

You are daughters of God. . . . You are made in the image of **our heavenly mother**. . . . Your body is sacred to you and precious. (In Conference Report, Mexico City and Central America Area Conference, 1973, p. 108)

One of our hymns, "O My Father," third verse, written by Eliza R. Snow, has beautiful words testifying of this truth (*Hymns of The Church of Jesus Christ of Latter-day Saints* [Salt Lake City, 1985], no. 292).

In the heav'ns are parents single?

No, the thought makes reason stare!

Truth is reason; truth eternal

Tells me **I've a mother there**.

And finally, in light of the doctrines of the plan of salvation, including the doctrine of celestial marriage leading to eternal families, it is certainly a matter of common sense that we would have a Mother in Heaven. Exaltation is for couples only. That means a husband and a wife. The Lord explained it this way in the Doctrine and Covenants:

D&C 132:19–20

19 And again, verily I say unto you, **if a man marry a wife** by my word, which is my law, and by the new and everlasting covenant, and it is sealed unto them by the Holy Spirit of promise, by him who is anointed, unto whom I have appointed this power and the keys of this priesthood; and it shall be said unto them—Ye shall come forth in the first resurrection; and if it be after the first resurrection, in the next resurrection; and shall inherit thrones, kingdoms, principalities, and powers, dominions, all heights and depths—then shall it be written in the Lamb's Book of Life, that he shall commit no murder whereby to shed innocent blood, and if ye abide in my covenant, and commit no murder whereby to shed innocent blood, it shall be done unto them in all things whatsoever my servant hath put upon them, in time, and through all eternity; and shall be of full force when they are out of the world; and they shall pass by the angels, and the gods, which are set there, **to their exaltation** and glory in all things, as hath been sealed upon their heads, **which glory shall be a fulness and a continuation of the seeds forever and ever** [*in other words, exaltation includes the joy of having and raising spirit children forever as husband and wife*].

20 Then shall **they be gods** [*the husband and the wife*], because they have no end; therefore shall they be from everlasting to everlasting, because they continue; **then shall they be above all**, because **all things are subject unto them. Then shall they be gods**, because **they have all power**, and **the angels are subject unto them.**

97

Question: What is a patriarchal blessing?

Answer: It is a blessing of prophetic counsel and guidance given to worthy members of the Church by an ordained patriarch.

It is a great blessing and privilege for a worthy member of the Church to receive his or her patriarchal blessing. It can be considered personal scripture for the recipient, a personal message from Heavenly Father. With rare exceptions, it is a one-time event. There is no set age requirement, but the candidate should be mature enough to respect and appreciate what this blessing is.

A patriarchal blessing should contain a declaration of lineage. It can contain blessings tailored specifically to the individual's needs, as well as prophecy about the person's potential in this life and the next. It includes warnings, things to be accomplished in life, difficulties to be overcome, talents and abilities to be developed and enjoyed, and many other things, depending on what the Spirit dictates to the patriarch.

The lineage, which is declared by the patriarch by direct revelation, reveals which tribe of Israel the person's blessings are to come through. The declaration of lineage is not a declaration of race or national origin. Rather, it is related to organizing and governing the kingdom of God. No matter which of the tribes of Israel is declared to be a person's lineage, they all include the blessings promised to Abraham, Isaac, and Jacob, which are the blessings of exaltation and the responsibility of helping the Lord take the precious gospel and priesthood ordinances to all the world (Abraham 2:9–11). Thus, when a person has been given a declaration of lineage in a patriarchal blessing, that member of the Church knows that he or she is capable of attaining exaltation, since Abraham, Isaac, and Jacob have already received their exaltation (D&C 132:29 and 37).

Patriarchal blessings can serve to encourage and uplift recipients and help them understand who they really are and what their potential is. If they are spiritually prepared to receive the blessing, they are left, at the end of the blessing, with a strong witness of the Holy Ghost as to their value and potential in the eyes of their Father in Heaven. This feeling and inspiration can remain with them throughout their lives and help them avoid evil and choose the right in order to avoid diminishing who they really are. In a very real way, the blessing illuminates his or her divine potential as it pertains to this life as well as the next, and serves, so to speak, as a personal "Liahona" to be referred to often throughout life.

As stated earlier, a patriarchal blessing sheds light on what the Lord has in store for that person. It can contain significant blessings, spiritual and often physical, that can strongly impact and strengthen the person throughout his or her life. Often, a patriarchal blessing will contain references to gifts of the Spirit possessed by the recipient or to be developed by him or her.

It is important to understand that once a patriarch places his hands upon the head of the person receiving the blessing, the line separating this life from the next often disappears. Thus, some blessings promised may not be fulfilled until the next life. But if the recipient strives to remain worthy, all the blessings relating to exaltation will be fulfilled.

It is also important to realize that a person's patriarchal blessing will not include everything that will take place in his or her life. Thus, if a major anticipated event such as mission or marriage is not mentioned in the blessing, it does not necessarily imply that it will not come to pass.

The receiving of blessings promised in patriarchal blessings is dependent upon personal worthiness. And, of course, the Atonement of Christ plays a vital role throughout a person's life in making possible ongoing worthiness or a return to worthiness as needed.

One's blessing is private and generally should be shared only with close family members or when the Spirit prompts to share it. It is appropriate to make extra copies to share with parents, spouse, or to carry with you. Many members put a digital copy on their electronic devices in order to have easy access to it and to make it easier to read often. In rereading a blessing often, over a lifetime, the recipient will find that certain parts of the blessing take on additional or changed meaning, depending on what stage of life he or she is in.

98

Question: How does one get a patriarchal blessing?

Answer: Get a recommend for a patriarchal blessing from the bishop or branch president and make an appointment with the patriarch.

The candidate for a patriarchal blessing, of course, should be striving to keep the commandments and thus be worthy of approaching Heavenly Father to obtain the blessing through a patriarch. The member makes an appointment with his or her bishop or branch president for a worthiness interview and to discuss getting a recommend for a patriarchal blessing. Once the recommend is obtained, the candidate contacts the patriarch and makes an appointment with him to receive the blessing. At the time of the appointment, the candidate should be spiritually prepared as best as possible and should be neatly groomed and in appropriate Sunday clothing.

99

Question: Is it true that if I sincerely repent, I will forget my sins?
Answer: No.

If one were to believe this, it would be discouraging and could lead to giving up on living the gospel or even hoping for salvation. It is true that, upon sincere repentance, the memory of serious sins can cease to occupy the mind on a daily basis, and, indeed, fade away such that they seldom come to mind. That is a tender mercy from the Lord and is one of the functions of the Holy Ghost as "the Comforter." But to believe or teach that you can know that you are forgiven only if you can no longer remember your sins is false. Alma the Younger is a prime example. His mentioning his past rebellion and grievous conduct to his son Helaman long after he had been forgiven is an excellent example of how past sins can be remembered in spite of repenting. In Alma, chapter 36, verses 12–17, Alma recounts his sinful past and the agonizing pain and suffering that initially racked his soul and led up to his repentance and, ultimately, to his being forgiven. Obviously, he can remember his sins. But the wonderful thing is that he is no longer in pain because of them. That is over. It is in the past because of the Atonement of Christ. His past mistakes no longer hold him prisoner. The pain has been replaced with exquisite, sweet joy.

Alma 36:19–22

19 And now, behold, when I thought this, **I could remember my pains no more**; yea, **I was harrowed up by the memory of my sins no more.**

20 And **oh, what joy, and what marvelous light I did behold**; yea, **my soul was filled with joy as exceeding as was my pain!**

21 Yea, I say unto you, my son, that **there could be nothing so exquisite and so bitter as were my pains.** Yea, and again I say unto you, my son, that **on the other hand, there can be nothing so exquisite and sweet as was my joy.**

22 Yea, **methought I saw**, even as our father Lehi saw, **God sitting upon his throne, surrounded with numberless concourses of angels,** in the attitude of singing and praising their God; yea, and **my soul did long to be there**.

Perhaps the reason some members of the Church misunderstand this issue is that they confuse the scripture in which the Lord states that when someone repents and has been forgiven, He, the Lord, no longer remembers their sins. They confuse His forgetting the sins with their own forgetting of sins.

D&C 58:42–43

42 Behold, he who has repented of his sins, the same is forgiven, and **I, the Lord, remember them no more**.

43 By this ye may know if a man repenteth of his sins—behold, he will confess them and forsake them.

100

Question: How and when are babies and young children tested who die before the years of accountability?

Answer: They are not.

A false rumor, which is often treated as doctrine, keeps coming around that these babies and young children will be tested at the end of the Millennium when Satan and his evil hosts are turned loose for the final battle, the battle of Gog and Magog (D&C 88:111–14). The reasoning behind this false doctrine seems to be that since these babies and children were never tested by the devil, they still have to undergo this. Joseph Fielding Smith taught that this is false doctrine.

Satan will be loosed to gather his forces after the millennium. The people who will be tempted will be people living on this earth, and they will have every opportunity to accept the gospel or reject it. **Satan will have nothing to do whatsoever with little children or grown people who have received their resurrection and entered into the celestial kingdom.**

Satan cannot tempt little children in this life, nor in the spirit world, nor after their resurrection. **Little children who die before reaching the years of accountability will not be tempted**: those born during the millennium, when Satan is bound and cannot tempt them, "shall grow up without sin unto salvation" (D&C 45:58). (*Doctrines of Salvation* [Salt Lake City: Bookcraft, 1955], pp. 56–57)

NOTES

NOTES

NOTES

ABOUT THE AUTHOR

David J. Ridges taught for the Church Educational System for thirty-five years. He taught adult religion and Know Your Religion classes for BYU Continuing Education and spoke at BYU Campus Education Week for many years. He has served as a curriculum writer for Sunday School, seminary, and institute of religion manuals. His callings in the Church include Gospel Doctrine teacher, bishop, stake president, and patriarch. He and his wife, Janette, have served two full-time Church Educational System missions. They are the parents of six children and are enjoying a growing number of grandchildren. They reside in Springville, Utah.

Scan to visit

www.davidjridges.com